MINISTRY FORMATION for EFFECTIVE LEADERSHIP

Ministry Formation for Effective Leadership

William R. Nelson

ABINGDON PRESS
Nashville

Ministry Formation for Effective Leadership

This book is printed on acid-free paper.

Library of Congress Cataloging-in-Publication Data

Nelson, William R. (William Rhame), 1930-
Ministry formation for effective leadership / William R. Nelson.
p. cm.
Bibliography: p.
ISBN 0-687-27038-3 (pbk. : alk. paper)
1. Clergy—Office. 2. Pastoral theology. 3. Christian leadership. I. Title.
BV660.2.N38 1988
253'.2—dc19
87-28408
CIP

MANUFACTURED BY THE PARTHENON PRESS AT
NASHVILLE, TENNESSEE, UNITED STATES OF AMERICA

To the memory of my father,

Warren Rufus Nelson,

whose general practitioner style of Chiropractic, without either of us knowing it, provided the model for my generalist approach to theological education.

CONTENTS

FOREWORD

I HAVE HAD THE PRIVILEGE OF PARTICIPATING AS A COLLEAGUE AND friend with William Nelson in the adventure of his formulating the point of view and building the structure of this book. It represents intensive discipline on his part and a prodigious amount of work as he has worked through several distillations and revisions to present to you as his reader the sustantive treatment of the stories of the power of God in the lives of Christian leaders. He has demonstrated competence as a Christian leader himself and shares his own struggles in spiritual formation in a clear, personal, and persuasive way.

The book is squarely set upon a solid biblical foundation. He interprets the primary data of the scripture in a fresh and vital way. He causes biblical leaders to "come alive" in the daily idiom of mine and your personal decision making as to the kinds of Christian leaders we are and with God's grace are enabled to become. The refreshing interpretations of the lives of early Christians make of them creatures like unto us and like whom we can aspire to become persons who are not too luminous and glorious for our daily emulation.

In addition to this, this book is an adventure in narrative, or story, theology. No neat divisions between sacred and secular let us "off the hook" of responsibility to God for our own clearcut choices and decision making as to what manner of Christian leader we have been called to be. He speaks to us holistically about our total response with our complete being.

As such, the book is a spiritual direction guidebook for individual reflection, for coagulating conversation in spiritual formation groups in seminaries, and for such conversations among working pastors who meet regularly in spiritual support groups. Whether you agree with Nelson or not is not his concern. Rather his primary interest is to engage you in vital self-direction in your pilgrimage.

The heart of the book seems to be its emphasis on the mentor relationship in the education and discipling of Christian leaders. This important ingredient of education has been all but automated out of our mass production assembly lines of "big" churches, "big" colleges and universities, and "big" seminaries. The cult of numbers has imperialized the very nature of religious experience. William Nelson's book is wholesome corrective, pointing us back to the way the Spirit of God takes the form of some very ordinary and fallible people to shape and form new generations of ministers of the gospel.

I commend the book as one useful in both schools and churches for both candidates for pastoral ordination and laypersons activating their daily work as a ministry in the name of Christ.

Wayne E. Oates, Ph.D.
Professor of Psychiatry and Behavioral Sciences
University of Louisville
School of Medicine
and
Senior Professor of Psychology of Religion
and Pastoral Care
The Southern Baptist Theological Seminary
Louisville, Kentucky

PREFACE

THE VARIOUS ASPECTS OF MINISTRY FORMATION ARE SO PERSONAL that they have been only rarely addressed formally. This book is intended to assist you in pursuing this highly personal process. My own ministry formation began with a young adult dream that was initially an acceptance of "the call to preach." When the role model shifted from pastor to professors, my vision was adjusted as "the call to teach." The latter version of my emerging dream went through several refinements as I have gotten in touch with my particular gifts and skills. In fact, the two versions merged as a call to seminary related theological field education, which has been complemented by regular involvement with chuch related pastoral ministry. An earlier book entitled *Journey Toward Renewal* documents the completion of my first decade of ministry formation. The insights of the past fifteen years will be shared in this update of my ongoing pilgrimage.

Appreciation is expressed to President William R. Myers and the Northern Baptist Theological Seminary Board of Trustees for the privilege of a sabbatical leave. My gratitude is also extended to President Roy L. Honeycutt and his colleagues at my alma mater, Southern Baptist Theological Seminary, for providing the residential context in which this book was conceived and initiated. The continuing guidance of Wayne E. Oates as a consultant during the writing process has been most helpful. Working closely with one of his students, Walter C. Jackson III, was invaluable during the research phase of the project. Also, Ronald F. Deering graciously made available to me the magnificent collection of the Boyce Centennial Library.

My wife, Colleen, deserves special mention for encouraging the project and for working around my absence. My colleagues, especially Dean David M. Scholer and E. Alfred Jenkins, have been sources of inspiration. My student assistants, Barry D. Lovett and John B. Newson, Jr., and my secretaries, Laura Thomas and Mary Choate, have offered devoted assistance. Gerald L. Bovchert, Douglas Choate, Rita Fox, and Robert C. Powell, M.D., also read the manuscript and offered helpful suggestions. Many others have touched my life in significant ways and have left indelible marks on my ministry formation. My hope is that this book will contribute to your ministry formation for the purpose of effective leadership.

William R. Nelson

Northern Baptist Theoloical Seminary
Lombard, IL

MINISTRY FORMATION
for
EFFECTIVE LEADERSHIP

INTRODUCTION

THE STORY OF A FOUNDERING SEMINARIAN WILL REMIND YOU OF the tentative way in which your ministry formation started. John invited me to become his mentor and has granted permission for me to share his story. He had just come to the realization that an M.Div. degree did not automatically guarantee placement in a church. Staying on for a further degree only compounded the problem. This twenty-nine-year-old male seminarian decided to volunteer his services in a nearby urban church. Washing dishes in a hospital had helped to put him through seminary, but his actual ministry experience was very limited. Working with the Children's Division of the Sunday school reminded him of a traumatic event that happened when he was four.

> I lost my balance at the head of the steps. It's hard to believe that I bounced from one step to another until I hit the banister near the bottom. The rebound caused me actually to bounce head-first into a large trash can at the foot of the steps. My mother later told me how she pulled me out and held me for about fifteen minutes until I stopped crying

That story describes his actual situation of being stuck in the seminary, waiting for someone to pull him out and get him into a church. When this rescue operation did not take place, he decided to withdraw officially from his advanced degree program. Working as a night watchman "tided him over" financially while he tried to find himself in a limited ministry experience.

A turning point for John came in recalling another childhood event that took place at the age of five.

> I remember the excitement of being told by my mother that a party had been planned to celebrate my birthday. At the time, I did not understand that it was still several weeks away. Instead, I went into the living room and waited patiently for the party to begin. After about twenty minutes, when nothing happened, I decided to leave the living room and go out into the yard to play.

It was a revelation to connect this story with his new church related ministry. Instead of waiting to be rescued, he had taken the initiative this time by withdrawing from seminary. The yard in which he was playing represents the nearby urban church. Getting in touch with his repressed playfulness is an unexpected by-product of working with the children in Sunday school.

John's preparation for ministry had been largely academic. He was just beginning to experience the connection between his unique personhood and his limited ministry performance. In other words, his own childhood stories helped him understand his initial experience of ministry formation.

Some working definitions will help you to appreciate the progress that you are making in your formation as a growing professional person. The term *ministry* is literally translated "service." The less familiar term *formation* (literally "bringing things together") suggests an internal shaping of your own approach to effective service. The combined expression "ministry formation" becomes a technical term for the processes that are chosen as your "support system for the enrichment of personhood and to assist in the performance of tasks."[1] In terms of ministry formation, the enrichment of personhood is the formation and the performance of tasks is the ministry.

The exercise of ministry formation takes place primarily through the processes of self-reflection and theological reflection during the course of engaging in the practice of ministry. You are the person who is primarily responsible for the process of "self-reflection." This phrase is understood as your capacity to learn from your own experience. As John has already illustrated, your own story is a major resource in helping you to understand and to interpret the critical events of your professional development.

Your ministry formation also includes "theological reflection." This expression broadens the scope of your reflection, because your Christian calling traces its roots to the revelation of God in history through Israel, Jesus Christ, and the ongoing Christian tradition. If "theology" is the study of God with the help of biblical and historical sources, then you also need to learn from the sources of the Christian faith. Theological reflection is not limited to the disciplines of historical and systematic theology. It also includes biblical studies and the entire history of the Church. In other words, theological reflection is another process of ministry formation by which you formulate your encounter with God's Word through the Scriptures, God's work through the Church, and God's people through your ministry.

Put yourself in John's situation, and I'll help you test your reflective capacity. He had been driven by a strong need for acceptable academic performance. This task was completed without allowing his personhood to develop at the same pace. His introverted personality tended to cause him to shy away from his peers and to stay within his own world. Perhaps the lack of placement in a church merely reinforced what he knew already. He would have to come out of his turtle shell and become more outgoing in order to "make it" in ministry. His imbalance was on the side of "getting the job done" in seminary—reading books, writing papers, listening to lectures, entering class discussions, and so on. The churches that were considering him expected a totally different kind of performance—reading Scripture, leading in prayer, preaching sermons, communicating enthusiasm in making announcements, and so on. Since he did not have an extroverted personality, John was willing to settle for a support role as an assistant pastor. It eventually dawned on John that he would not have an opportunity to play even "second fiddle." Instead, he found a modest church position as a volunteer on his own initiative. He felt the need to work under the guidance of a seasoned urban pastor who would help him find a balance between *being* and *doing* in ministry. The assignment of working with children reduced the threat level so that he could concentrate on expressing himself more freely.

The new setting for the enrichment of John's personhood enabled him to build self-confidence and to feel better about his self-worth. He was beginning to understand his placement impasse as the consequence of his own limited ministry formation. The process of critical self-reflection was enhanced by interaction with the senior pastor, who was able to push his theological reflection from the implicit to the explicit level. Of course, the starting point of John's ministry formation was a reality test of his actual situation. The different kind of performance expectations between the seminary and the church were recognized. The new ministry with children was providing a context for the enrichment of John's personhood. The picture was now clear in terms of where he had been as a seminary student, where he is in an initial ministry experience, and where he is going in future church placement. John concurs that the stages of his development are illustrated by three graphs (see fig. 1).

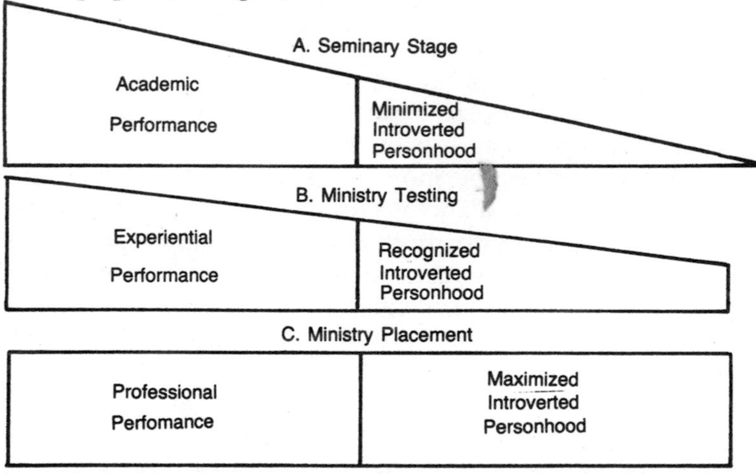

John's Perception of His Ministry Formation (fig. 1)

The past performance of academic-experiential imbalance was ended by his withdrawal from seminary. The present period of experimentation was beginning in an urban church setting. The future hope of church placement would depend on reaching the goal of a more balanced, professional integration of performance and personhood.

This book is an invitation for you to join with me in examining the balancing act of what it means "to do" ministry and at the same time "to be" God's person. The storytelling approach for getting at this balance requires the critical capacities of self-reflection. Both processes of "doing" and "being" begin in the present, draw on the past, and create the future. You will be encouraged to look back over the milestones that have brought you to the present stage of your ministry formation. The goal of this self-help manual, however, is to sharpen your vision for looking ahead. Identifying some of the issues that need to be resolved will make you more aware of achievable goals for your ongoing ministry formation.

Seizing the initiative to engage in your own ministry formation cannot take place in a vacuum. Both your limitations and your uniqueness make you different from all other ministers. You are "one of a kind" to such an extent that communication becomes a high risk adventure. Sometimes it seems better to "play it safe" by keeping your personal goal for effective ministry to yourself. Yet you really do want to know what significant others *think* about your ministry goal—that is evaluation. Perhaps you would also like to know what these persons *feel* about your style of interpersonal relationships—that is feedback. Otherwise, you are left guessing on the basis of what others choose to *do* in relation to your ministry. They join with you enthusiastically, half-heartedly, or not at all.

The purpose of theological and self-reflection is to help you become a more effective church leader. Seven stories will be presented, which deal with the struggle of getting started in the Christian ministry. The biblical stories were told before they were written. They have in common a sense of divine guidance that will help you become more aware of the need for ministry formation. The other, more recent, stories are from verbal and written sources. They will put you in touch with persons whose ministry formation emerges from the hot ashes of apparent failure.

The unifying theme of this book is the sharing of stories. By drawing on biblical, historical, and contemporary stories, you will learn how others who have preceded you in ministry join with you in the quest for evaluation, feedback, and support. Clarification and confirmation of your goal for ministry formation will emerge as you reflect on the variety of ministry models that follow. The following summary of the various stories will help you determine the key issues in your ministry formation.

If you are still in seminary, the biblical story of John Mark will make you more aware of your limitations at the beginning of your ministry formation (chapter 1). You will have a natural affinity with John Mark, whose "minor billing" in the book of Acts will be elevated to "star status." Having responded to at least a tentative Christian calling, you will recognize your cautious beginning in the story of this young minister. You may be fortunate in having the supportive role model of a senior colleague. Then, you will appreciate the special part that Barnabas plays in the ministry formation of his nephew.

Perhaps you are already engaged in ministry on a part- or full-time basis. The biblical stories of Peter, Stephen, and Paul will dramatize your unique strength as a professional church leader (chapter 2). (It may not be as clear why Peter, Stephen, and Paul are singled out from among all the other leaders of the early Church. You will learn how Luke[2] uses them to personify the narrative structure of the book of Acts.) The remarkable variety of ministry models that are contained in these three stories presented by Luke in the book of Acts will help you to recognize your uniqueness. The empathetic style of Peter suggests that the raw material of your person centered orientation can be put to good use in pastoral ministry. The efficient style of Stephen implies that your goal orientation may need to be tempered by the demands of your situation. The integrative and effective style of Paul infers that God can build on all of your previous experience as "grist for the mill" of church leadership.

The recognition of your uniqueness will help you to identify the leadership style that is your natural gift for ministry. A woman in ministry, Betty Hochstetler, of Chicago, has a natural affinity for the empathetic leadership style of Peter (chapter 3). The Mennonite congregation that she served as co-pastor, along with her husband, Lee, reenacts the biblical dynamics of the book of Acts. If you are a natural empathetic leader, this leadership style will be recognized as you reflect on her story.

Involvement in another vocation before entering the ministry calls for a career change. Augustine of Hippo had this experience and will help you to confirm your pastoral identity (chapter 4). The choice of Augustine as a towering figure in the entire history of the Church provides a bridge between the distant biblical prototypes and the contemporary ministry models. The formative years of Augustine's life, as presented in his *Confessions,* will enable you to evaluate the way in which the outer layers of other vocational options can be peeled off. Inside there must be congruence between your Christian calling and your professional identity. It is not enough to determine whether your dominant leadership style tends toward empathetic "being," efficient "doing," or an effective balance of both. The Augustinian quest for pastoral identity demonstrates the need for an integration of "the mind and the soul" (being) with "the will" (doing).

Your initial ministry involvement may not go according to a preconceived master plan. Wayne E. Oates, of Louisville, revised his initial plan. He will help you to negotiate a course correction that will intensify your spiritual formation (chapter 5). A major disappointment in his early teaching career will help you to utilize "the school of hard knocks" as an unexpected, but essential, curriculum for your spiritual growth. The Augustinian influence on Professor Oates' approach to spirituality will give you a working model for accelerating this aspect of your ministry formation. Like

Pastor Betty, a spotlight is turned on the reality of a painful experience that God used to enrich and confirm Professor Oates' goal for effective leadership.

The use of a storytelling method for focusing your ministry formation is reinforced by the relatively new discipline of narrative theology. Biography and autobiography are prominent ways in which "the story of [your] life" may be told. Because your story may be recalled only in "bits and pieces," autobiography is the key to the particular stories that have been selected to illustrate your ministry formation. Getting in touch with your story is essential if you are planning not only to survive, but also to succeed in a largely mentorless environment. This manual for theological and self-reflection will become a mirror in which you may see yourself more clearly and find the courage to articulate the goals that will continue to guide your ministry formation.

The progression of these seven stories represents the unavoidable issues of ministry formation during the first decade of your professional development: identification of your *limitations*, recognition of your *uniqueness*, refinement of your *pastoral leadership*, integration of your *pastoral identity*, and acceleration of your *spiritual formation*. Reflecting on your limitations and your uniqueness may serve as a review of your past experiences in ministry. Working ahead to your leadership style, your professional identity, and your spiritual formation will follow. These predictable crises of young adult development lie ahead on your pathway to becoming a more effective minister.

The challenge of "being" God's person in the ministry requires a high degree of purposeful self-motivation and reflective criticism. Reflecting on these stories is an exercise in self-discipline that will enable you to clarify the goal toward which you are moving in your early ministerial career. Questions at the end of each chapter will help you to clarify many aspects of your story.

The relationship between your story and self-reflection on your ministry formation may be unconnected in your experience up to this point. Whether you are male or female, some preliminary questions will start you thinking about the kind of church leader that you want to become.

What is the impetus that motivated your Christian calling? What is the goal that presently guides your ministry formation? Is it a dedication to the study of the Bible, church history, or Christian theology in order to become a more effective teacher? Is it a passion to reform the structures that control our society in order to make it possible for all persons to become truly human? Is it a desire to build up the body of Christ as a reconciling community of faith for the purpose of evangelizing the world? The critical capacity for self-reflection will help you to articulate the goals that you will set on the way to becoming an effective pastoral leader.

Reflection oriented to the past will turn your attention to the search for authenic ministry models in Scripture and in church history. Your own pastoral identity and spiritual formation will become issues for your reflection in the present. The resulting goals that anticipate the future will become a projection of the balance that is prescribed for your own effective leadership in ministry. You are invited to join me in moving from the past, through the present, and into the future with the help of the stories that follow.

CHAPTER ONE

IDENTIFYING YOUR LIMITATIONS: *JOHN MARK*

Imagine yourself standing on Mount Washington in Pittsburgh, observing the coming together of the Monongahela and the Allegheny Rivers to form the Ohio River. The two rivers that join to form the Ohio River can be distinguished no longer in the single new stream. Your story is that ongoing River of Life, which draws from the River of Facts and the River of Meaning. The single, new stream could be called the River of Interpretation because "the story of [your] life" is the interpretation that you give to the interaction of facts and meaning.

The objective *facts* of your story are obvious. They include your age, sex, marital status, family background, home church, educational accomplishments, and special interests. It is not so easy to describe the subjective *meaning* of your story. This is where you will need to use the processes of theological and self-reflection. The interplay of facts and meaning becomes the *interpretation* you give to "the story of [your] life."

You have gone swimming on many occasions in the River of Facts. You can describe the external part of your story with considerable ease, but there is still a mystery connected with the River of Meaning, which causes you to "stay put" and enjoy the view from a safe distance. The internal part of your story is in flux and needs the refinement that will come from self-reflection and theological reflection. This chapter will give you guidance so that you will have the courage to jump into the River of Meaning. It is from that direction that you will enter the River of Interpretation, which is the destination toward which your ministry formation is leading.

Every young minister needs an interpretative framework for understanding his or her strengths and weaknesses as a Christian leader. One way of moving toward the River of Interpretation is to make an honest assessment of your limitations. The biblical story of John Mark's ministry formation will help you to get in touch with your limitations. A careful distinction will be made between the *facts*, as presented in the book of Acts, and the *meaning* that this biblical narrative might have for your ministry formation. It is natural to begin with the story of an ambivalent young minister, whose entrance into ministry is more like a roller coaster ride than a clearly marked trail.

JOHN MARK'S FACTUAL REALITY

Among the heroes of the early church, one of the minor characters deserves to be featured. The aspiring young minister, John Mark, moved in and out of the action that centered around Barnabas and Saul during the first and second missionary journeys. Reading Acts 12–15 will refresh your memory on this part of the history of earliest Christianity.

Like most young ministers, John Mark's story began as an eager young Christian who was nurtured by his "home church" in Jerusalem. The meeting place was the house that he shared with his mother, Mary (Acts 12:12). Presumably, his mother was a widow and a woman of substance. This inside association with the apostles made him an eligible traveling companion for the early Christian missionaries. His uncle, Barnabas, was a wealthy Jewish believer from Cyprus, whose generosity was demonstrated by the gift of some land to the church at Jerusalem (Acts 4:36-37). He is remembered as the Jerusalem church leader who went out of his way to recruit the recently converted Pharisee, Saul, for the first missionary team (Acts 11:22-26). He also recruited John Mark for this missionary team while Barnabas was on a visit to Jerusalem with Saul (Acts 12:25).

The bare facts of John Mark's roller coaster pattern of ministry formation will be summarized on the basis of the storytelling approach that Luke takes in presenting the history of earliest Christianity.

> In the church at Antioch . . . they placed their hands on them [Barnabas and Saul] and sent them off. . . . John [Mark] was with them as their helper. . . . From Paphos, Paul and his companions sailed to Perga in Pamphylia, where John [Mark] left them to return to Jerusalem. . . . Some time later Paul said to Barnabas, "Let us go back and visit the brothers in all the towns where we preached the word of the Lord and see how they are doing." Barnabas wanted to take John, also called Mark, with them, but Paul did not think it wise to take him, because he had deserted them in Pamphylia and had not continued with them in the work. They had such a sharp disagreement that they parted company. Barnabas took Mark and sailed for Cyprus, but Paul chose Silas and left, commended by the brothers to the grace of the Lord. (Acts 13:1, 3, 5*b*, 13; 15:36-40)

This story of ministry formation is part of the "sending off" of the first missionary team from Antioch, introducing Luke's Mission narrative (Acts 13:1–28:31). (Luke's concluding section is in contrast to the Tradition narrative—Acts 1:1–6:7. It is made possible by the Transition narrative—Acts 6:8–12:25.) More will be said about the overall literary framework of Luke's second volume, which is inseparable from his Gospel, in the next two chapters. For now, the focus will be kept on John Mark's story.

The support role of one who goes along "to help" Barnabas and Saul suggests that John Mark's primary loyalty was to his uncle Barnabas (Colossians 4:10). The identification of the team as "Barnabas and Saul" implies that the church at Antioch viewed Barnabas, the respected emissary from the Jerusalem church, as the team leader. The newcomer, Saul, was incorporated into the team primarily on the recommendation of Barnabas. John Mark was clearly in a subservient position, the starting point of formation for most ministers.

A closer look at Acts 13:5*b* (literally "And they had John as helper") may reveal a working title for this young minister who was embarking on his first ministry assignment. The term "helper" is used for Christian ministers here; also, in Acts 26:16, it appears as "servant." Both translations imply a secondary, or subservient, position.[1] The literal "rowing under" image suggests a lowly slave on the lowest of the three banks of oars inside a Roman galley. On a good day, John Mark may have felt like a "minister" (KJV) or "assistant" (NEB); on a bad day, the title "general flunky" (CPV) probably seemed more appropriate.

Now for the shock! The enthusiasm with which John Mark began his initial ministry experience came to an abrupt end when he decided to "leave them to return to Jerusalem" (Acts 13:13*b*). The precise reason or reasons for his withdrawal have prompted many speculations, but no theory can be presented with certainty. The best approach to this mystery is to look for the answer in relation to John Mark's quest for meaning as a young minister. That inquiry needs the background of the remaining facts of the story.

Barnabas' nickname, "Son of Encouragement" (Acts 4:36), was given concrete expression by his recommendation of John Mark to Paul as a useful participant in the second missionary journey (Acts 15:37). Paul's veto of the suggestion was based on the previous pattern of desertion (Acts 15:38). The result is "a sharp disagreement" between Paul and Barnabas, which caused them to go their separate ways. Barnabas took John Mark to his home territory of Cyprus, and Paul took Silas to the new frontiers of missionary service in Asia Minor and beyond (Acts 15:39-40). There is no evidence that Paul and Barnabas ever met face-to-face again. Paul later softened his approach to John Mark when he wrote from a Roman prison: "Only Luke is with me. Get Mark and bring him with you, because he is helpful to me in my ministry" (II Timothy 4:11; see Philemon 24 and Colossians 4:10). Second- and third-century tradition connected Mark with the Gospel that bears his name and attested to a closer relationship to Peter than to Paul. The hesitant minister who eventually "made good" may have veiled an autobiographical reference to himself by adding the unusual detail about the young man who fled away naked in the Garden of Gethsemane (Mark 14:51-52). If John Mark were the evangelist, it is significant that he was the first to put the oral tradition about Jesus into the literary form known as "Gospel." The action oriented account, which is the briefest of the four Gospels, seems to be consistent with the tradition that Papias records to the effect that Mark "had neither heard the Lord nor been his personal follower."[2]

The uncertainty about the possible happy ending of this story need not cloud the factual record of John Mark's ministry formation. In short, he initially starts out high and ends up low. When he tried to start up again, he encountered rejection from one early church leader and experienced continuing support from the other. The actual reality of his external history, however, does not tell the whole story. Imagination will be used to reconstruct an interpretative framework of meaning, which will help you to get in touch with your own internal history.

JOHN MARK'S SEARCH FOR MEANING

Experiences like those of John Mark are commonplace in the early stage of ministry formation. The events leading up to his desertion from the first missionary team, when it reached the coast of Asia Minor, will place that turning point within a broader context.

A sigh of relief must have been breathed when John Mark learned that their initial destination beyond Antioch would be Cyprus, the familiar island from which his uncle had come to Jerusalem (Acts 4:36). The uneventful journey from Syrian Antioch led to the port city of Seleucia, sixteen miles away (Acts 13:4). From Seleucia, they embarked on a ship and sailed about 130 miles to Salamis, the main harbor for the island of Cyprus. Their destination was the official residence of the Roman Proconsul, Sergius Paulus. What awaited them in Paphos was not at all what John Mark expected. Instead of a polite welcome and pleasant meal, the missionaries were met by an obnoxious magician and false prophet named Bar-Jesus (Acts 13:6-8).

In a dramatic turn of events, the subdued Saul became the assertive Paul, who rose to the occasion with a defensive rebuttal against Bar-Jesus, which left both Barnabas and John Mark speechless. The missionary purpose of the converted Pharisee, Saul, is presented with such eloquence that Luke chose to use the Roman name, Paul, for the first time in his account of Paul's ministry (Acts 13:9). Paul's feisty and combatant defense of the Christian faith succeeded in subduing the sorcerer Bar-Jesus (Acts 13:10-11). Luke reports the results in an ambiguous comment, "When the proconsul saw what had happened, he believed, for he was amazed at the teaching about the Lord" (Acts 13:12). Whether he believed in Christ or in Paul's authority to defeat the court magician is not made clear.

The Reality Test of Identity

The emergence of Paul as the spokesman for the missionary team seemed to overshadow the earlier leadership role of Barnabas. It certainly left John Mark wondering to whom he was accountable. The primary role of Barnabas on the missionary team of "Barnabas and Saul" (Acts 13:2) was giving way to the reorganized team of "Paul and his companions" (Acts 13:13*a*). This sudden change of leadership created a vacuum in which John Mark also had doubts about his own identity as an aspiring young minister. Perhaps his search for meaning at this point was related to an awareness of his limitations. He was beyond his depth. Was his decision to desert the missionary team at Perga in Pamphylia an act of self-assertion (Acts 13:13*b*)? Did he need time and space to allow his ministry formation to catch up with the demands of his ministry context? Was he intimidated by the confidence and competence of Paul? Frank Stagg speaks for the "underdog":

> Paul was as susceptible to error as was Mark. It may be that the *courage* of Mark enabled him to turn back at Perga. Possibly Mark left because he dared to live his own life. Mark's life achievements may have been made possible by escape from the dominating, if not domineering, personality of Paul.[3]

John Mark realized rather quickly that he was not ready for Paul's stringent demands and his passionate commitment to a Gentile mission. John Mark's maturity had not developed to the point of keeping up with this kind of performance expectation. A realistic assessment of his own limitations required further work on his identity formation. This reconstruction of the biblical dynamics may help you to become more intentional about your ministry formation.

Resolving the tension between identity formation and role diffusion is the primary task of young adulthood. In this connection, John Mark must have imagined himself saying to Paul as they sailed from Cyprus to Perga:

> Now, Brother Paul, you are moving too fast for me. When we started out on this trip, I thought that we would be working in the home territory of Uncle Barnabas, but your plans are far beyond what I am willing to risk. Am I supposed to renegotiate my field education contract in mid-stream? I had no idea that you would become my supervisor. My mind is set on the limited assignment made by my uncle. Now you expect me to go with you to far-away Galatia in Asia Minor. I've heard about the strange "Lycaonians" and the other characters up there in the hills of Lystra and Derbe. They are not "my kind of people." I have had enough!

Does this young minister with a tentative ministerial identity and the subservient role of "general flunky" want to slow down his ministry formation? Instead of trying to "fake it" beyond his proven ability, John Mark should be commended for identifying his limitation. An awareness of identity diffusion called forth his *assertion of independence.* Paul, and perhaps Barnabas, may have been ready for an advanced course in cross-cultural missionary service, but John Mark was not.

The Reality Test of Spirituality

When identity formation is examined within a ministerial context, it merges with faith development. The belief system that John Mark acquired within his Jewish/Christian orientation was not adequate for the faith challenge of an emerging Gentile mission. This young minister was shocked by Paul's "power encounter" with the sorcerer Bar-Jesus. The gutsy language of Clarence Jordan presents the full impact of this clash between the forces of good and evil:

> You crooked creep! You low-down louse! You son of the devil! You full-time phony! You habitually twist God's clear message out of shape. All right now, listen, the Lord has put *the* finger on you and you'll be as blind as a bat for some time. (Acts 13:10-11*a* CPV)[4]

As an innocent bystander at Paul's dramatic encounter with the devil, John Mark must have drawn back and said, "I didn't mean to register for this course."

This shocking introduction to Paul's super-assertive ministry style was not the only problem. John Mark also had his whole upbringing in the Jewish heritage challenged when the governor of Cyprus, Sergius Paulus, responded positively to Paul's ministry. Ambivalence about a threatened belief system could not be ignored on the voyage to Asia Minor. Before expressing his intention to leave the first missionary team, an imaginary "show down" with his new supervisor can be reconstructed.

> Brother Paul, what do you think you are doing? I have been trained as a Hebrew. Do you honestly believe that we can bring these "Gentile dogs" into our common faith? I'm not as sure as you seem to be. I need some time to talk with the elders in Jerusalem in order to get excited about your new vision. Are you building a new organization that leaves behind the tradition of Jesus? Have you forgotten that he was a Jew?

Was a crisis of faith churning inside this reluctant young minister when he announced his decision to leave Perga and return to Jerusalem? The tentativeness of faith development called for his *assertion of self-direction*. He had decided to "set the pace" of his ministry formation on a more gradual course.

The Reality Test of Authority

The conflict within John Mark was accentuated by both the supervisory authority that was exerted by Paul and this young minister's lack of self-assurance. The zealous Pharisee, who had been converted on the Damascus Road, now became an authority figure with whom both Barnabas and John Mark had to interact. The same charismatic personality who had worked against the presumed Messiah was now working for the risen Christ as "Paul and his companions" (Acts 13:13*a*). Luke initially presented Paul as a compulsive missionary strategist whose leadership style was task oriented in contrast to the person centered style of Barnabas. John Mark wanted to say to Paul on that voyage to the mainland of Asia Minor:

> Brother Paul, let me give you a piece of my mind. When we started out from Antioch, I thought that Uncle Barnabas was in charge. Now that you have taken over, I have had it with your "heavy-handed" approach. You wonder why I am not intimidated by your leadership. You must have thought that I could adjust to whatever happened, but I am not going to be the "lowest rower in the boat" when you were not appointed as the captain of the ship!

Mark's original commitment to Barnabas and his hesitation to go any further with Paul may be understood as his *assertion of family loyalty*. The pace that he wanted to set for his ministry formation was more compatible with the low-key approach of Barnabas than the high-powered tactics of Paul.

Three developmental tensions within this aspiring young minister provided him the confidence to become his own person by taking a stand against the aggressive style of Paul. His departure was an exercise in self-assertion, in which he gained the time and space for strengthening his particular gifts before proceeding any further on his ministerial journey. You may have experienced this predictable entry crisis of young adulthood by getting "over your head" in ministry, as I did, before even entering seminary. You may be in the early stage of contemplating a lifelong commitment to Christian ministry. You may want to withdraw from a less satisfying vocation in order to become a minister. You may be tempted to assume the role of full-time pastor immediately, without taking the time for a theological education or a period of apprenticeship with a more experienced colleague. Like John Mark, reassessing your options and pacing your ministry formation may be appropriate at this stage of your personal growth and professional development.

ASSESSING YOUR LIMITATIONS

You have already begun to connect the actual events of your ministry formation with the unavoidable entry level issues of identity diffusion, faith development, and pastoral authority. The factual markers along your ministerial journey are embedded in an interpretative framework that gives meaning to your life. The beginning of your ministry will be aided by the reality test of identifying the limitations that are inherent in these developmental issues.

Your Identity Diffusion

The identity issue of early adulthood is one of Erik H. Erikson's eight stages of being.[5] Stage five is the pivotal identity crisis that assimilates the earlier stages of trust, autonomy, initiative, and industry. It also opens the door to the subsequent stages of intimacy, generativity, and integrity.

How would you answer the question, "Who am I?" Where are you on the spectrum between fidelity to the task you envision as your particular calling and identity diffusion that leads to indecision? Identity diffusion is defined as "a split of self-images . . . a loss of center and a dispersion."[6] John Mark's crisis of withdrawal from the first missionary team is predictable from this perspective. The uncertainity about his role on the team activated feelings of identity diffusion, which undermined his self-confidence. Without understanding Mark's struggle, Paul interpreted his departure as a lack of commitment to the mission of Jesus. Barnabas was sensitive to his nephew's need to work on the nature of his particular calling. In fact, Barnabas' willingness to give Mark a second chance even took priority over his continuing relationship with Paul. You will be fortunate to have the encouragement of a more experienced colleague during the course of your early professional development.

If you are a woman entering ministry, a corrective is needed to the male developmental perspectives of Erikson. Carol Gilligan insists on more flexibility in the life-cycle dynamics of women in ministry:

> While for men, identity precedes intimacy and generativity in the optimal cycle of human separation and attachment, for women these tasks seem instead to be fused. Intimacy goes along with identity as the female comes to know herself as she is known, through her relationships with others.[7]

Unlike the stages of faith development that follow, your progression through the stages of being is gender specific. The male tendency to move from identity toward intimacy is in contrast to the usual female preference for allowing identity to emerge in a relationship of intimacy with another person. Recognizing your gender, you should take this developmental difference into consideration.

Your Faith Development

Like identity, your faith is also a growing and developing phenomenon. This assessment will be aided by the interpretative framework of five stages of knowing/valuing.[8] Your viewing ministry formation from a developmental perspective may be confusing when entering the realm of faith. You are conditioned to believe that this human response to the gift of God's grace is beyond analysis and should only be acknowledged with thanksgiving. Yet the pre-conditions of faith, from a theological perspective, include the experiential environment of your earliest relationships and the affiliative support of your early religious training.

The five stages may be characterized as intuitive, literal, conventional, reflective, and paradoxical. Your faith development builds on the foundation of what you learned *intuitively* from your parents, what you learned *literally* in your early religious training, and what you assimilated more *conventionally* from the belief system of your home church and denominational tradition. Next comes the stage of integrating *reflectively* these earlier stages into your own religious experience. The stage of recognizing the *paradoxically* conflicting tensions within your faith is the goal toward which most persons aspire.

A summary of these five stages in simplified relational language will help you to assess the progress of your faith development:

1. "God's just like my mommy and daddy" [Intuitive-Projective Faith];
2. "What's fair is fair" [Mythical-Literal Faith];
3. "I believe what the church believes" [Synthetic-Conventional Faith];
4. "As I see it, God . . ." [Individual-Reflective Faith]; and
5. "Don't confuse the map with the territory" [Paradoxical-Consolidative Faith].[9]

The gap between the ideal "map" in the Scriptures and the real "territory" as you experience it in ministry becomes the paradox that still has to be admitted and reconciled.

John Mark's struggle illustrates two of these stages that are an unavoidable part of ministry formation. The pre-conditioning of his earlier Jerusalem training was in conflict with the new challenge of missionary service. His recognition of this limitation was internalized as a feeling of inadequacy. John Mark became immobilized by the tension between his conventional Jerusalem orientation, which was grounded in Jewish tradition (stage 3), and the need for a more reflective orientation that included openness to the Gentile mission (stage 4). There was an enormous gap between his more conventional faith (stage 3) and the seemingly paradoxical faith of Paul, which accepted the differences between Jewish and Gentile believers (stage 5).

From the perspective of faith development, the pressure is really on John Mark. You also may be caught between the tension of your family/home church background and the reflective demands of "in-service" training during your theological education. Likewise, your faith perspective must be more than a representation of your parents' faith and the belief system of their denominational tradition. It must grow out of your own reflective faith, which expresses your individuality apart from your earlier experiential/affiliative conditioning. Identifying your limitations includes an assessment of the extent to which you are moving beyond the easy acceptance of the faith of your primary nurturers (father, mother, or pastor) and of your nurturing community of believers to your own reflective faith. The more paradoxical faith of Paul, which allowed for the reconciliation of opposites, provides a clue concerning what lies ahead in your further spiritual formation for ministry.

Your Pastoral Authority

Your own pastoral authority is the third developmental issue that needs assessing at the beginning of your ministry. Obviously, it grows out of your emerging personal identity and the current stage of your faith development. Yet, you may need to examine the source of your "authority." This elusive term cannot be defined purely in psychological terms as "the ability to affect, influence, and change other persons."[10] In Christian ministry, it becomes a theological concept. Authority is granted in contrast to power, which is usurped. The God-given quality of "pastoral authority" is the supervision (literally, "oversight") that is bestowed on a minister for the purpose of affecting, influencing, and changing both persons and congregations. Authority is bestowed immediately, but it has to be earned relationally. Henry Mitchell offers helpful advice to the beginning minister: "Don't use your authority until you've got it."

What can be used, when it is appropriate, can also be abused. If your authority is not rooted in the pastoral office, it will degenerate into raw power, which is the unbridled and intentional control of persons and congregations.

The tension between God-given external authority and your own internalization of that authority cannot be separated. The distinction in narrative theology between external and internal history is useful in this connection. The revelation of God that reaches its climax in the facts of the Christ event is your external history. The meaning that you give to this external reality in your own life becomes your Christian identity, or your internal history.

Your internal authority is put to the test in ministry, because you become the "medium" through which the "message" is communicated. Marshall McLuhan argues that messages undergo subtle changes of meaning when transmitted through different channels. Whether the channel is a human being or a wide range of media, to a large extent "the medium is the message." H. Richard Niebuhr applies this principle to the interdependence of external and internal history: "We are in history as the fish is in water and what we mean by the revelation of God can be indicated only as we point through the medium in which we live."[11] Your internal authority becomes the *medium* through which the external authority of God's message is communicated. Your appropriation of God's *message* changes the medium through which it is shared with others.

Therefore, your pastoral authority is both external and internal. It represents the merging of the God-given River of Facts with the internalized River of Meaning to form the united River of Interpretation. The river of external authority is the objective record of God's revelation in Scripture and his continuing presence in the Church through the Holy Spirit. The other river of internal authority is your perception and appropriation by faith of these realities. The resulting merger is "the story of [your] life," the interpretation that becomes your pastoral authority. The merging of these two rivers leads H. Richard Niebuhr to "speak of revelation only in connection with [your] story."[12]

John Mark's departure from the first missionary team can be used as a story for reflecting theologically on the authority issue. Paul inadvertently sets himself up as an authority figure in his "power encounter" with the sorcerer Bar-Jesus. Paul's authority was rooted in his Pharisaic loyalty to God's message. It had the unconscious effect of making John Mark aware of the limited internal authority that was present in the medium of his Jewish Christian faith. Therefore, it was not surprising that John Mark chose to distance himelf from Paul, perhaps for the purpose of strengthening his own internal authority. An awareness of this limitation in your early ministry formation is based on the extent to which the message of God's external authority finds a natural expression through the medium of your internal authority.

By reality testing your ministry formation, you may expose a deficiency in one or more of these developmental issues. An assessment of your formation in relation to these issues is itself a positive step forward. The particular facts that make up your story are also subject to more than one level of meaning. Now, you should have a clearer picture of the limitations that inhibit you from moving into the future.

Roger Palms' affirmation that *God Holds Your Tomorrows* includes a helpful exercise for moving toward the goals that will become your agenda for ministry formation.

> Think back five years. Would you have dreamed five years ago that you might be where you are now, doing what you are doing today? Would you have anticipated the world events or economic changes that are happening now? . . . We can't anticipate our tomorrows. The misery of the unbeliever is that he has to try, because he does not know the One who owns tomorrow. But the believer does, and even though he (or she) cannot see the future, he knows that the God who owns him also owns that future.[13]

Whether your particular ministry is still anticipated or is already in process, you are moving toward the goal of God's tomorrow with a heightened awareness of your own limitations.

The roller coaster pattern of John Mark's ministry formation is not exactly the same as your experience. The external facts may be different, but you must deal with the three same internal issues of meaning. Your self-reflection is related largely to *the identity issue.* Your theological reflection puts a spotlight on *the faith issue.* The interaction of your faith and identity point to *the authority issue.* An honest assessment of these issues will dramatize the limitations that must be overcome during the course of your ongoing ministry formation. These "growing edges" will need to be identified so that specific goals can be set for your professional development.

You may have identified with some aspects of John Mark's struggle. Now "the shoe is on the other foot." The following questions will assist you in making the application to your own situation. Then you will be ready to continue making progress on the marked trail of your ministry formation with an examination of your style of leadership. The identification of any possible weaknesses will be balanced by the recognition of your natural strength as a Christian leader.

Questions for Self-reflection

1. Have you experienced a big responsibility in ministry, like John Mark, for which you were not fully prepared? How did you avoid your superiors' accusation of your having deserted the post of duty?

2. Is experience by itself really the best teacher, or do you feel the need for a stronger theory base as the foundation of your ministry formation? How would you interpret the need to make an intentional shift from superficial *action* to a period of extended *reflection?*

3. Can you identify with a developmental interpretation of John Mark's departure? How does it feel to be a "general flunky"?

4. Do you agree with John Mark's decision to leave the missionary team? Would you seek to make the best of a bad situation or to risk the misunderstanding of a more drastic decision?

5. What limitations have you experienced in relation to the current stage of your identity formation?

6. Do you feel like a pastor inside your being, or are you doing the work of a pastor in the hope that a stronger sense of professional identity will emerge?

Questions for Theological Reflection

1. Are you considering a vocational commitment to the Christian ministry? Will it require deserting another job?

2. How would you articulate your experience of Christian calling? Did it emerge gradually within a Chrisitian home, or was it a more dramatic experience?

3. How would you describe the current stage of your faith development? Can you describe the difference between your present stage and the previous one?

4. How is your pastoral authority related to the external authority of the revelation of God in Scripture? What is the relationship between your internal authority and this external authority?

5. What does it mean to say that "the medium is the message"? What is the message? What is the medium?

6. Do you have any responsibility for guiding other persons into the realm of theological reflection? Does your pastoral authority help you to view your leadership role in ministry as that of a practicing theologian?

CHAPTER TWO

RECOGNIZING YOUR UNIQUENESS: *PETER, STEPHEN, AND PAUL*

THE SOPHISTICATION OF MODERN ELECTRONICS INCLUDES A scanning device on the sound system of many new cars. When the scan button is pushed, the dial of the AM/FM tuner moves systematically to each station within receiving distance. It stops for a few seconds of transmission on each station and continues until the stop button is pressed. Let me introduce you to the key biblical narratives in the book of Acts by scanning for the most important stories. If your imaginary dial consists of the twenty-eight chapters of Acts, the scan will reveal certain patterns of repetition and length that single out the stories of Peter, Stephen, and Paul.

First of all, you notice that the scan stops twice on Peter's story dealing with the conversion of Cornelius (Acts 10 and 11:1-18). You are startled by two stations that are transmitting the same signal. Another scan reveals an unusually long transmission on Stephen's story of trial defense and martyrdom (Acts 7). This station is most conspicuous. It is the longest signal of the twenty-four speeches or sermons in the book of Acts. Even more surprising, the scan stops three times for the conversion of Paul (Acts 9, 22, and 26). The threefold repetition of the same signal makes an impression that stimulates your curiosity.

This scanning device enables the reader to identify three episodes that are featured in Luke's storytelling approach to the history of earliest Christianity. These pivotal stories are: the reluctant involvement of Peter in the conversion of the Gentile named Cornelius, the catalytic role of Stephen in the launching of the Gentile mission, and the reversal of roles from persecutor to propagator in the conversion of Paul.

Everybody likes a story. Even history can be told in story form. Storytelling is the key to Luke's literary method.[1] The stories that have special significance in Luke's literary account of the first three decades of the early Church are the fast-moving events that evolve around Peter, Stephen, and Paul.

These key stories will be discussed in a different order from their presentation in Luke's historical narrative on the basis of their relationship to the larger literary structure of the book of Acts. Peter's story is oriented to the *past* and epitomizes the Tradition narrative (Acts 1:1–6:7). Stephen's story places you in the *present* and personifies the Transition narrative (Acts 6:8–12:25). Paul's story looks ahead to the *future* and embodies the Mission narrative (Acts 13:1–28:31).

This chapter will introduce you to three biblical models of pastoral leadership. Peter's story suggests a backward look at the reality of your previous training. Stephen's story will confront you with a deeper awareness of your present situation. Paul's story will stimulate a projection of the future goal toward which you are moving. In addition to connecting your ministry formation with the past, present, and future, these stories will help you to appreciate your uniqueness. You may be naturally inclined, like Peter, to center your ministry in working with people, or you may be more goal oriented, like Stephen, and find your greatest satisfaction in developing programs. You are indeed fortunate, like Paul, if you are already finding a balance between the personhood and performance aspects of ministry.

Your entrance into the ministry may resemble one or more of these leadership styles. The three biblical stories of Peter, Stephen, and Paul will provide windows through which you may see more clearly the natural way of exercising pastoral leadership. Any adjustments that are required in your leadership style, by either your recognition of imbalance and/or your need for further growth, will put this item on your agenda for ministry formation.

PETER'S STORY OF FORMATION

The sources for studying Peter's role in the New Testament are: Paul's letters, the book of Acts, the four Gospels, and Peters' letters. This inquiry into Peter's ministry model will be limited to Luke's perspective. The first half of the book of Acts is the primary source, since Peter is not mentioned after Acts 15. A recent ecumenical assessment suggests that Luke presents Peter as:

— a *preacher* in the Jerusalem church, a missionary preacher to outsiders, and a spokesman for the Christian community;
— a *miracle worker* [whose] miracles resemble those of Jesus in the Gospel accounts; and
— an *object of miraculous divine care* [who] receives heavenly guidance.[2]

According to the biblical account of that group of Twelve closest to Jesus during his earthly ministry, Peter was the only one to move beyond a national outlook. Peter's shift from the narrowness of his Jewish training to the acceptance of a world mission came to a turning point in Acts 10–11. Like Peter, you, also, are influenced by all the past experiences that have contributed to your formation. Therefore, you will be sympathetic to the difficulty with which Peter adjusted to the new reality of the Gentile mission.

Preliminary hints of a Gentile mission are contained in the spontaneous scattering of the Hellenist followers of Stephen (Acts 8:4) and in the preaching of the Hellenist Philip (Acts 8:5:13, 26-40). (The Hellenists were Greek-speaking Jewish Christians.) Philip's witness among the despised "half-breed" Samaritans and to the black eunuch from Ethiopia built upon the momentum of Stephen's preaching. Whether the eunuch was a Jew or a "God-fearing" Gentile is not clear. That doubt is removed in relation to the Roman centurion, Cornelius. Luke specifically calls him "devout and God-fearing" (Acts 10:2*a*). The designation "God-fearing" was reserved for Gentiles who were favorable to Judaism and already observed many Jewish practices. It is significant that Cornelius was not only a Gentile but also a Roman. The mission to this influential Gentile was reserved for Peter.

The dramatic way in which Luke describes this event suggests that it is God's intention for the Gentile mission to be blessed by one of the original apostles. The spontaneous preaching to Gentiles in Antioch (Acts 11:19-21) and Paul's extensive mission to the Gentiles began *after* Peter's decisive action.[3] Grounding the Gentile mission in the authority of Jerusalem, of which Peter was a leading representative, related this event to the Tradition narrative (Acts 1:1–6:7). The fact that Cornelius was also a Roman anticipated the replacement of Jerusalem by Rome at the end of the Mission narrative (Acts 13:1–28:31).

Listening to an Inner Voice

The way in which God prepared Peter for this new chapter of ministry was in the realm of his internal history. The first account of Peter's trance-vision is presented with vivid imagery, which becomes a way of listening to God.

> About noon the following day as they were on their journey and approaching the city, Peter went up on the roof to pray. He became hungry and wanted something to eat, and while the meal was being prepared, he fell into a trance. He saw heaven opened and something like a large sheet being let down to earth by its four corners. It contained all kinds of four-footed animals, as well as reptiles of the earth and birds of the air. Then a voice told him, "Get up, Peter. Kill and eat."
>
> "Surely not, Lord!" Peter replied. "I have never eaten anything impure or unclean."
>
> The voice spoke to him a second time, "Do not call anything impure that God has made clean."
>
> This happened three times, and immediately the sheet was taken back to heaven. (Acts 10:9-16)

This trance-vision is distinguishable from a dream only by the state of being awake, not asleep. In this revelatory experience, Luke identifies Peter as a "Jew" (Acts 10:28) who was confronted by God with his own cultural conditioning.

The second account of the trance-vision (Acts 11:4-10) is presented in relation to a defense in Jerusalem of Peter's precedent-breaking openness to the Gentiles.

Renegotiating the Grip of the Past

The internal conflict that Peter needed to renegotiate involved an experience of chronic loss.[4] Peter had to separate himself from the emotional ties that were deeply embedded in his Jewish consciousness. From this perspective, his trance-vision is akin to a bereavement experience that moves through predictable stages. Separation from the restraints of his Jewishness needed to be dealt with as an experience of chronic loss before he could be able to accept the new reality of a Gentile mission.

The context of Peter's trance-vision is not coincidental. Anyone who was familiar with the story of Jonah would be pre-conditioned, perhaps unconsciously, to associate the seaport of Joppa with the avoidance of mission to the Gentiles (Jonah 1:3). Peter wrestled with that same impulse to *deny* the Gentile mission in his trance-vision.

An immediate *angry* response by Peter to the command of the inner voice to eat is also predictable. He could not even consider eating unclean animals that were on the forbidden list of every Jewish person (Leviticus 11). It was only a short step from resisting "unclean" food to having reservations about relating to persons who were "impure" (non-Jewish or alien). Peter's negative response came straight from his feeling of revulsion and was verbalized in the angry outburst: "Surely not, Lord! . . . I have never eaten anything impure or unclean."[5]

An implicit attitude of *bargaining* is expressed in the repetition of the voice a second and a third time: "Do not call anything impure that God has made clean." The mental debate continued until the "sheet" was pulled up again into heaven. Peter's trance-vision merely brings into sharper focus an ongoing process of renegotiating the restraints of his Jewish particularism.[6]

Confusion, perhaps bordering on discouragement and *depression,* is implied in the subsequent events of Peter's story. Not only was he "wondering about the meaning of the vision" (Acts 10:17*a*), but he was also immobilized when the emissaries from Cornelius "stopped at the gate" and "called out" (Acts 10:17*b*-18). Another vision was necessary to prompt him to "get up and go downstairs" and "not hesitate to go with them . . . " (Acts 10:20). Peter's difficulty in moving beyond his entrenchment in Jewish tradition is impressed on the reader by means of the literary technique of reiteration. The continuing intrusion of the angel's visit (Acts 10:22, 30; 11:13) served as a reminder that it was God who was pushing Peter to renegotiate the next phase of his ministry.[7]

Acceptance emerged during the slow process of "acting out" the meaning of the vision. It began as Peter extended hospitality to his Gentile visitors: "Then Peter invited the men into the house to be his guests" (Acts 10:23*a*). It continued with his entering the house of Cornelius in Caesarea (Acts 10:23*b*-27). His personal reflection brought confirmation that the vision dealt not only with food laws but also with human relationships: "But God has shown me that I should not call any man impure or unclean. . . . I now realize how true it is that God does not show favoritism" (Acts 10:28*b*, 34*b*). The descent of the Holy Spirit upon the entire household of Cornelius puts God's own stamp of approval on Peter's acceptance of the Gentiles (Acts 10:44-48). Luke intended for the reader to understand that Cornelius was more than a "token" Gentile; an entire (Gentile!) congregation was founded in his home.

Lest you think that your own past experience can be renegotiated without an ongoing struggle, Paul presented a "footnote" on Luke's account of Peter's ministry formation. Galatians 2:11-14 describes a regression to Peter's old behavior pattern. In Antioch, the presence of Jewish Christian visitors from Jerusalem caused Peter to withdraw from Gentile table fellowship. Paul's chagrin at this is expressed in his letter to the Galatians. F. F. Bruce defends Peter's apparent inconsistency: "He would have claimed that he acted out a consideration for weaker brethren—the weaker brethren on this occasion being those back home in Jerusalem."[8] This early example of "situation ethics" suggests that Peter's formative pattern for renegotiating ministry is an ongoing process that reveals his empathy for both Jews and Gentiles. He was in the priestly tradition of the Old Testament, in which the primary emphasis was on meeting the spiritual needs of people.[9] It did not matter whether they were Gentiles or Jews. He was faithful to the institutional church in Jerusalem and, as the spokesman of the Twelve, was willing to extend his priestly function to all persons, regardless of race or nationality.

Modeling an Empathetic Leadership Style

Peter's ability to respond to the deepest needs of both Gentiles and Jews is not inconsistent or inappropriate. It reflects an empathetic leadership style that stresses personal relationships more than organizational goals. Like Barnabas, Peter was a natural encourager once he became personally related to individuals who needed his non-directive support. His strength emerged from the center of his *being*, rather than from the outward accomplishments of his *doing*. His natural leadership style found expression in openness to those in need, regardless of their nationality or ethnic backgrounds. Your identification with Peter's leadership style may be similar to mine; instead of a trance-vision in broad daylight, I had a similar revelatory experience in a dream at night.

My sabbatical leave in Louisville ended with a reentry dream, outlining the agenda that awaited my return to Nothern Baptist Theological Seminary. The dream took me to a regular chapel service, at which I was scheduled to preach. During the opening hymn, President William R. Myers handed me a note. It explained that his introduction would refer to my recent sabbatical experience as a spiritual journey. David Augsburger, a former faculty colleague, had returned in order to lead in prayer. When it was my turn to speak, I found myself standing behind the pulpit, speechless. I suddenly became aware of an embarrassing situation. My shoes and my socks and my Bible were missing. Without an explanation, a quick exit to the conference room downstairs did not turn up the missing items. Fortunately, my search was not conducted alone, since my present faculty colleague, E. Alfred Jenkins, came downstairs with me. Instead of finding what we were looking for, we found a room full of trash. Six bundles were picked up and fastened to a coat rack. During this hurried effort, my thoughts were turned away from the chapel service upstairs to my own search for wholeness. As if fighting a battle with the certainty of a victorious climax, an assurance came over me that "the enemy" was really going to be defeated by this clean-up campaign.

The images and persons in this dream are significant to my ongoing ministry formation.

> The "barefoot in the pulpit" image symbolizes my own inward journey during the sabbatical leave. The "intuitive-feeling" side of my personality is being strengthened while the "extroverted-judging" side is being subdued.[10] The six bundles of trash represent the incompleteness of this task.
>
> The presence of other persons in the dream indicates that I am not alone on the journey. President Myers' identification with spiritual formation confirms my empathetic leadership style toward which I am moving.[11] David Augsburger represents the earlier struggle of subduing an efficient leadership style from which I am coming.[12] Alfred Jenkins is the faculty colleague who was present with me during this time of transition.
>
> The "clean-up" image suggests that ministry formation is an ongoing and incomplete process of growth and change. Working together with another person on cleaning up the trash in both of our lives is the name of the game. My senior colleague, Alfred Jenkins, has been that kind of "companion on the inner way."[13]

Peter's ministry formation included a serendipitous experience of renegotiating his previous ministerial training. My sabbatical leave ended with an important dream. My need is to continue moving away from goal oriented efficiency toward a more disciplined approach of person centered empathetic leadership.

Your uniqueness will become more apparent when you examine the inertia that limits your ministry formation because of past pre-conditioning. Whether it is the limitation of Peter's Jewishness or of my goal orientation, this aspect of your search for meaning may be called a "coming *from*" pattern of ministry formation. It forces you to become more aware of the cultural and interpersonal forces that have brought you to your present stage of identity formation and faith development. The backward look of Peter's ministry model calls for an integration of your past tradition with your present reality. Jerusalem is not the same as Joppa. Peter's story will help you update your ministry formation and test your leadership style. Renegotiating the background from which you have come, however, is not the end. It is a means to the end of facilitating a more empathetic leadership style in the present.

STEPHEN'S STORY OF CONFRONTATION

Stephen's story, which is told only in the book of Acts, is introduced at the end of the Tradition narrative (Acts 6:1-6). Luke lists him first among "seven men from among you who are known to be full of the Spirit and wisdom" along with Philip and the others (Acts 6:3). Stephen is described as "a man full of faith and of the Holy Spirit" (Acts 6:5). His Christian calling, along with that of six of his Greek-speaking Jewish Christian colleagues, was recognized and confirmed by the Jerusalem church. The Seven were appointed "to wait on" (*diakonein*) tables (Acts 6:2). At this point, their task was ministry. (The use of the Greek verb from which "deacon" is derived does not yet suggest a specific office in the church.) The Seven were initially concerned with meeting human needs among the Greek-speaking widows. Their appointment to engage in ministry was aimed at enabling the apostles to "give [their] attention to prayer and the ministry of the word" (Acts 6:4). Yet, it is ironic that these Grecian Jews, not the apostles, were the first to preach, and to practice, a mission to the Gentiles that was not hindered by Jewish tradition.

Luke concludes the Tradition narrative with a summary statement (Acts 6:7), which leads to the beginning of the Transition narrative: "Now Stephen, a man full of God's grace and power, did great wonders and miraculous signs among the people" (Acts 6:8). His practice of ministry met with immediate opposition among the Greek-speaking Jews of Jerusalem (Acts 6:9-12). They were offended not by his charitable deeds but by his threatening words: "This fellow never stops speaking against this holy place and against the law" (Acts 6:13). They retaliated by asking for an explanation of his blasphemy before the Sanhedrin (Acts 6:15-7:1).

Challenging the Religious Establishment

Stephen's long sermon (Acts 7:2-53) is an expanded statement of the early Church and moves beyond the cultural boundaries of Christian Judaism to claim an inclusive world mission. His overview of the entire history of Israel reaches its climax in a scathing renunciation of the man-made institutions of the Temple: "But it was Solomon who built the house for [God]. However, the Most High does not live in houses made by men" (Acts 7:47-48). Stephen's frontal assault was on the principal structure of Judaism. His radical position was more than a plea for a spiritual temple with a spiritual priesthood and spiritual sacrifices. It was also an accusation that the Temple had been a mistake from the beginning. Stephen's denunciation sounded completely subversive. He was in the prophetic tradition of the Old Testament, in which the emphasis is on speaking the truth that was revealed by God, regardless of the consequences.[14] This charismatic leadership style was in conflict with the status quo of the Jewish religious establishment. As an efficient church leader who "tells it like it is," he clearly prefered the earlier, mobile style of the Tabernacle (literally, "tent of meeting"). He could only see the Temple as an Herodian perversion of the original intention of God, which was lost in the formalities of a fixed institution.

The fierce bite of Stephen's attack on the Jewish establishment was met with an even more violent reaction. His conviction before the supreme court on a charge of blasphemy led to his immediate execution by stoning. It was followed by the dispersal of his fellow Hellenists, who were believed to share his unorthodox views. Stephen's insistence on confronting the religious establishment led to his sudden death.

> When they [the council] heard this, they were furious and gnashed their teeth at him. But Stephen, full of the Holy Spirit, looked up to heaven and saw the glory of God, and Jesus standing at the right hand of God. "Look," he said, "I see heaven open and the Son of Man standing at the right hand of God."
>
> At this they covered their ears and, yelling at the top of their voices, they all rushed at him, dragged him out of the city and began to stone him. Meanwhile, the witnesses laid their clothes at the feet of a young man named Saul.
>
> While they were stoning him, Stephen prayed, "Lord Jesus, receive my spirit." Then he fell on his knees and cried out, "Lord, do not hold this sin against them." When he had said this, he fell asleep.
>
> And Saul was there, giving approval to his death.
>
> On that day a great persecution broke out against the church at Jerusalem, and all except the apostles were scattered throughout Judea and Samaria. (Acts 7:54–8:1)

The climax of Stephen's story is not the end of life for one faithful "witness" (*martyria*) but the beginning of mission for many faithful witnesses. The reference to "the Son of Man *standing* at the right hand of God" (Acts 7:56) is a triumphant word of victory in contrast to the usual "sitting" in this exalted position beside the heavenly Father (Matthew 26:64; Mark 14:62).[15] With the added excitement of Jesus' standing to cheer on the courage of his faithful servant, the early Church was inadvertently launched on its world mission.

Reinterpreting the Present Reality

The sense of loss, which resulted from Stephen's courageous action, may seem to be negative. Yet, the hindsight of theological reflection views it as overwhelmingly positive. The tragedy of one untimely death by stoning led the early Church to the triumph of spreading the gospel beyond Jerusalem for the first time on a large scale. The message is clear: "When God closes a door, he opens a window" (see fig. 2). The negative parts of Stephen's story—martyrdom, scattering, and persecution—became transformed into the positive spreading of the gospel "throughout Judea and Samaria" (Acts 8:1*b*) and subsequently to Antioch (Acts 11:19-21). Quite unintentionally, the reality of the harsh persecution led the Greek-speaking followers of Stephen to implement *by default* the missionary vision of the risen Christ, which had been given *by design*.

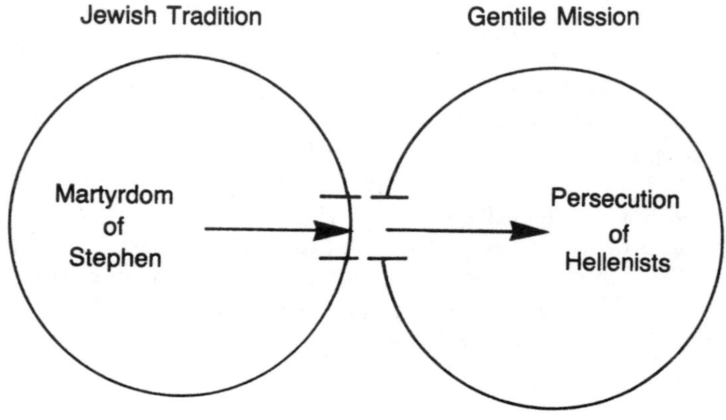

Stephen's Story of Confrontation (fig. 2)

The ripples that spread from the persecution of the Hellenists included Philip's preaching in Samaria and his witness to the Ethiopian eunuch (Acts 8:4-40). Lest the influence of the first Christian martyr be overlooked in

Antioch, Luke connected the same scattering with the preaching of the gospel "to Greeks also" in the cosmopolitan Syrian city on the Orontes River (Acts 11:19-21). The unnamed persons from Cyprus and Cyrene moved beyond the comfortable task of "telling the message only to Jews" and risked the bold new venture of speaking to "Greeks" [*Hellēnes*] also" (Acts 11:19-20). The pivotal reference to "Greeks" (Gentiles) was softened to read "Hellenists" (*Hellēnistai*) by some ancient authorities and is maintained in the latest Greek New Testament. The difficulty of moving beyond the Jewish-Christian connotation of "Hellenists" is illustrated by this textual problem. Instead of reserving the Gentile mission proper for Paul, Ernst Haenchen insists that "the contrast to 'Jews' requires rather 'Gentiles' " (*Hellēnes*).[16] This breakthrough in Syrian Antioch is a fitting tribute to the "working *through*" of Stephen's story of confrontation.

In contrast to Peter's "coming *from*" pattern, Stephen set in motion the Transition dynamics to get from "here" (Tradition) to "there" (Mission). Stephen's martyrdom, like Peter's trance-vision, was presented by Luke within the framework of the Transition narrative. Your place of service in ministry is likely "in the gap" between Tradition and Mission. The important learning from Stephen is the necessity of "transition." It is the process of movement from one stage of development to another. The transitional stories that Luke chooses present the movement of the early Church from Tradition to Mission. They also suggest that a reinterpretation of your present reality is the window through which you are able to view your goal for ministry formation in the future.

Modeling an Efficient Leadership Style

Stephen's single focus on confronting and changing the Jewish captivity of the early Church may be described as an efficient, though costly, leadership style. The task was accomplished, even though he did not survive to receive praise for launching the early Church on its world mission. This prophetic approach to leadership works best in emergency situations that require an emphasis on *doing*. Goals are put ahead of persons; production becomes more important than relationships. You may recall situations in which Stephen's task oriented leadership style was demanded. The difficult circumstances in which you sometimes find yourself may call for drastic action. These are exceptional situations that should occur rarely and should be dealt with carefully.

Is your natural leadership style unbalanced in the direction of empathy or efficiency? Either direction will work well in specific situations that require an emphasis on either *being* or *doing* as the circumstances dictate. An assessment of the style you most often use will help you to determine if your personal authority is expressed more naturally in working with people or in implementing programs. Achieving a more effective, balanced style is a worthy goal for the first decade of your ministry formation. The goal of finding the balance between *doing* and *being* will be represented by the integrated leadership style of Paul.

PAUL'S STORY OF TRANSFORMATION

The sources for the study of Paul in the New Testament are primarily his own letters and the book of Acts. In contrast to Peter, who is prominent in Acts 1–12, Paul is the leading figure in Acts 13–28. His efficient leadership style has been identified already in John Mark's story in connection with the first missionary journey. Yet, the fuller presentation that Luke gives of the premier missionary strategist of the early Church suggests that he also incorporated an empathetic leadership style. When it was no longer possible for Paul to work with John Mark and Barnabas, he began again with Silas (Acts 15:40). Paul had goals, but he also preferred a team approach. The intentional combination of both styles in Paul suggests that he is a biblical model of effective leadership.

A closer look at Paul's master story, which is told first in the Transition narrative, reveals another way in which Luke sets the stage for mission. A seemingly insignificant person is singled out in the crowd at the stoning of Stephen. Luke is careful to report that "a young man named Saul" was the one at whose feet the killers of Stephen threw their clothes (Acts 7:58). He had journeyed from Asia Minor in order to continue his rabbinical training with advanced study in Jerusalem. The young rabbi was becoming a zealous Pharisee in the school of Gamaliel, grandson of the famous Hillel.

Saul was neither revulsed nor neutral during the stoning of Stephen; he was actually "giving approval to his death" (Acts 8:1*a*). This brutal and clumsy form of violence was aimed at preserving the truth of the Torah. Yet, Saul's own dogmatic assurance was shaken by the way in which Stephen's death verified the central Christian belief, that Jesus, who had died, was alive and exalted in glory. The martyr's last words were spoken with his dying breaths: "Look . . . I see heaven open and the Son of Man standing at the right hand of God. . . . Lord Jesus, receive my spirit. . . . Lord, do not hold this sin against them" (Acts 7:56, 59-60*a*). Augustine observed that "the Church owes St. Paul to the prayers of Stephen." Saul could not escape the memory of Stephen's eyes and the mysterious communion with some living Spirit whom he called by Jesus' name. The martyrdom of one whose "face was like the face of an angel" (Acts 6:15) prepared the young man named Saul for the dramatic encounter with the risen Christ, which was a high point in the history of earliest Christianity.

Rearranging the Present Reality

Luke's first account of Paul's transformation is the classic model of Christian calling:

> As he neared Damascus on his journey, suddenly a light from heaven flashed around him. He fell to the ground and heard a voice say to him, "Saul, Saul, why do you persecute me?"
>
> "Who are you, Lord?" Saul asked.
>
> "I am Jesus, whom you are persecuting," he replied. "Now get up and go into the city, and you will be told what you must do."
>
> The men traveling with Saul stood there speechless; they

> heard the sound but did not see anyone. Saul got up from the ground, but when he opened his eyes he could see nothing. So they led him by the hand into Damascus. For three days he was blind, and did not eat or drink anything. (Acts 9:3-9)

The second and third accounts (Acts 22:6-11 and 26:12-19) add some interesting details. The "light from heaven" (Acts 9:3) was also "a bright light from heaven" (Acts 22:6) and "a light from heaven, brighter than the sun" (Acts 26:13), in which Saul saw the figure of Jesus, even though his companions saw only a formless glare. The short dialogue that follows is expanded in the third account:

> "Saul, Saul, why do you persecute me? It is hard for you to kick against the goads."
>
> "Then I asked, 'Who are you, Lord?'
>
> " 'I am Jesus, whom you are persecuting,' the Lord replied. 'Now get up and stand on you feet. I have appeared to you to appoint you as a servant and as a witness of what you have seen of me and what I will show you. I will rescue you from your own people and from the Gentiles. I am sending you to them to open their eyes and turn them from darkness to light, and from the power of Satan to God, so that they may receive forgiveness of sins and a place among those who are sanctified by faith in me.' " (Acts 26:14*b*, 15-18)

The "goads" were sharp-pointed sticks that were used to prod an ox at the plow. They were intended to hurt the animal that resisted, just as the zeal with which Saul persecuted the early believers actually hurt him. This ancient proverb from agricultural life says that "it hurts you to kick against the goads" (Acts 26:14*b* RSV). Paul was struggling with the conviction that the Christian case was true. The goads pricked his conscience as he watched Stephen's death, and they actually caused him to increase his resistance against the new movement. During this "screaming and kicking" mood, the risen Christ broke into Paul's consciousness with undeniable power: "I am Jesus, whom you are persecuting" (Acts 26:15*b*)—the Jesus whom you are kicking, and in this process you are really hurting yourself instead.

Paul's submission to the risen Christ is a dramatic version of the Christian calling. It builds on the great prophetic calls of Isaiah, Jeremiah, and Ezekiel. This dramatic experience, which is generally understood as conversion, is best described as a Christian calling of *transformation;* the latter word means "to change in nature, disposition, heart, and the like." The suddenness of Christ's encounter results in a complete "about face" or "change of heart."[17] Therefore, Paul's transformation is more than conversion; it is actually the classic model of Christian calling.[18]

Grasping a Dream for the Future

If formation is largely a process of reshaping the past, then transformation is akin to creating the future. The uniqueness of your Christian calling may lean in the direction of slowly renegotiating your past or of suddenly acknowledging the recreation of your future. A recent example of the latter pattern is James E. Loder, who builds on Paul's Damascus event:

> Saul's Damascus vision was a powerful mediating Presence that brought with it both a negation of his previous circumstances and the conviction that the answers to life's deepest questions were packed into that moment even before he had formulated any questions beyond the first, "Who are you, Lord?"[19]

You will identify with the dramatic way in which Christ encountered Paul if your calling into the Christian ministry emerged from a "transforming moment." For example, Loder describes a life-threatening automobile accident as the beginning event that enabled him to experience the need for ordination in the Presbyterian Church. As if echoing the impact of Stephen's death on Saul, he writes about his own convictional experience with unavoidable urgency:

> Although I resisted the implications of this experience [of near death in an automobile accident] for over two years, the

> eventual consequence was that I had to act on the growing necessity to identify myself with the ministry of the church and to complete the ordination proceedings.[20]

The turning point is a change within himself, which Loder describes as "the moment . . . that he was 'seen,' known, and understood, even in ways he had not been able to understand himself."[21]

The turning point for Paul was the change of direction from the pessimism of a persecutor to the optimism of a propagator. The first account of his "transforming moment" concludes with the intervention of an unknown believer named Ananias. God used Ananias to complete the work that he started in the death of Stephen and continued on the Damascus Road (Acts 9:10-19). Paul's transformative story may be summarized as "a vision, then blindness (negative healing), then the dream of Ananias' prayer and Paul's extra-sensory perception, and finally a healing in which Ananias lays his hands upon Paul."[22] The healing touch of Ananias and the reconciling words "Brother Saul" (Acts 9:17) turn the trauma of blindness into the tranquility of a new vocation. God used Ananias to define Paul's Christian calling as "my chosen instrument to carry my name before the Gentiles and their kings and before the people of Israel" (Acts 9:15*b*).

The efficient way in which Paul's story begins emphasizes the goal of persecuting the early believers. The rest of his story in the book of Acts presents the effective way he subsequently evangelized the world. Whether he was before the angry mob in Jerusalem (Acts 22) or the Roman official Agrippa in Caesarea (Acts 26), Luke presents Paul as a tireless missionary strategist who will not rest until he reaches Rome. Paul's strength and humility are in the kingly tradition of the Old Testament, in which leadership is based on divine guidance.[23] Paul is the model of the religious characteristics of the Israelite conception of kingship, which go beyond the political realm. His kingly style is effective because it is both prophetic and priestly. His efficiency is rooted in the charismatic inspiration of a prophet. His empathy emerges from the official functioning of a priest. Ideally, your goal for Christian leadership should integrate the Israelite conception of a prophet and priest who exhibits enough religious integrity to be designated as a king.

Modeling an Effective Leadership Style

The totality of Paul's transformation goes to the depth of his being and redirects the drive of his doing. The unfolding story of the early Church in the book of Acts describes his effective role as the apostle to the Gentiles. Notwithstanding his initial lack of empathy with John Mark, Luke's record of three missionary journeys and the trip to Rome presents the picture of an integrated leadership style. The balance between doing and being is quickly harnessed to the long-range goal of preaching in Rome. The efficient and empathetic leadership styles of Paul became effective, but this desirable balance did not come without a continuing struggle. A "thorn in [his] flesh" (II Corinthians 12:7) is a constant reminder of the necessity for continual dependence on God as the true source of his personal authority. This less confident picture is given by Paul himself. He admitted to an ongoing struggle, which he viewed as God's own way of keeping him "from becoming conceited because of these surpassingly great revelations" (II Corinthians 12:7). His bodily weakness is conjectured to be chronic ophthalmia, a condition that may have been aggravated by the blinding light from heaven on the Damascus Road (Galatians 4:15). Our remaining uncertain about Paul's "thorn," however, is preferable so that we can fill in the blank with our own struggle.

Nevertheless, the transformation that began in the Damascus event continued to help Paul find an effective balance between doing and being. If you can identify with the boundless energy of Paul, then his story confronts you with the realization that doing is not an end in itself but a means to the end of being a whole person in the acting out of your Christian calling. The slogan on a boot-shaped paperweight—"Do something: lead, follow, or get out of the way!"—is not enough. The essence of Paul's transformative story puts a spotlight on *being* God's person and *doing* God's will as an effective leader.

Like Peter, Stephen, and Paul, your ministry formation draws on an understanding of your past influences, on an awareness of your present reality, and on an openness to your future possibilities. Your leadership style may have an affinity to one or more of the Old Testament prototypes that are updated in Luke's master stories (see fig. 3).

Old Testament Prototypes	Luke's Master Stories	Your Leadership Style
Priest	Peter	Empathetic
Prophet	Stephen	Efficient
King	Paul	Effective

Selecting Your Leadership Style (fig. 3)

Like Peter, if you have a natural gift for working with people, you are an empathetic leader. Based on the need for negotation in most situations, you will want to consider the appropriateness of remaining an efficient leader, such as Stephen, if administration is your natural gift. Particular situations of injustice or emergency will force you to become a prophet; yet, the combination of patience and persistence that is present in an effective leader, such as Paul, is obviously preferable. Ideally, the balanced style of effective leadership combines the characteristics of prophet, priest, and king.

Building on Your Unqiue Strength

Recognizing your natural gift as a church leader is one way of determining your unique strength. The descriptive terms *empathetic*, *efficient*, and *effective* are more than abstract labels because they are personified by three biblical models. The three key leaders in Luke's storytelling approach to the history of the early Church do not start "from scratch." They exemplify the primary types of leadership in the history of Israel: *priest, prophet,* and *king*. Whether you are attracted to the contemporary management terms or the ancient biblical types, each provides you with a vocabulary for describing your own leadership style. Now you are beginning to build on your strength as an empathetic priest, as an efficient prophet, and/or as an effective king.

Again, Luke's account of the early Church is useful because it requires you to connect your strength as a church leader with the past, with the present, and with the future. This process of ministry formation, like Luke's master stories in the book of Acts, points in particular ways to the climactic adverb *unhindered* (Acts 28:31 RSV). Peter became a reformed "priest" who conquered national pride. Stephen was a confrontative prophet who became a witness unto death. Paul was transformed by an experience of blindness into a kingly missionary who is valued also as a prophet and a priest.

Likewise, your renegotiation of past tradition, your involvement in present reality, and your openness to future possibilities are aimed at unhindering your effectiveness as a professional church leader. This formation process is as ancient as the three stages of classical Greek drama—exposition, conflict, and resolution. Luke's biblical drama of the early Church presents the three stages as Tradition, Transition, and Mission. The goal of becoming an effective leader, like Luke's purpose statement (Luke 24:46-48; Acts 1:8), is more than a geographical program for your career development. It is also an opportunity for developing cross-cultural and interracial sensitivity. Effective ministry needs to model a balance between geographic outreach and cultural inclusiveness. The crossing of cultural barriers in word and deed requires the necessity of reaching out "to all nations [*ethnē*]"(Luke 24:47). Luke's master stories illustrate the power that is released in three persons who reach out "to all ethnics" with their own unique strength as early Church leaders.

Instead of viewing your career in terms of particular geographic locations, Luke challenges you to become engaged in cross-cultural ministry. If your goal for effective ministry does not include an openness to ethnic diversity, you will want to read the book of Acts again from this perspective.[24]

In scanning Luke's master stories from the perspective of your unique strength, you will find that two observations are useful. First, you will identify initially with all three of the ministry models. You want the scan to continue from one story to another so that your goal for effective ministry can incorporate each one. You are always in the process of "coming from" the past, of "working through" the present, and of "going to" the future. You resist touching the "stop" button on the scan. Like a typical congregation, you have contained within yourself the effects of your past heritage and the aspiration of reaching contemporary goals. Lyle E. Schaller's diagram of these opposite orientations within a local congregation may be viewed as a picture of your ministry formation (see fig. 4).[25]

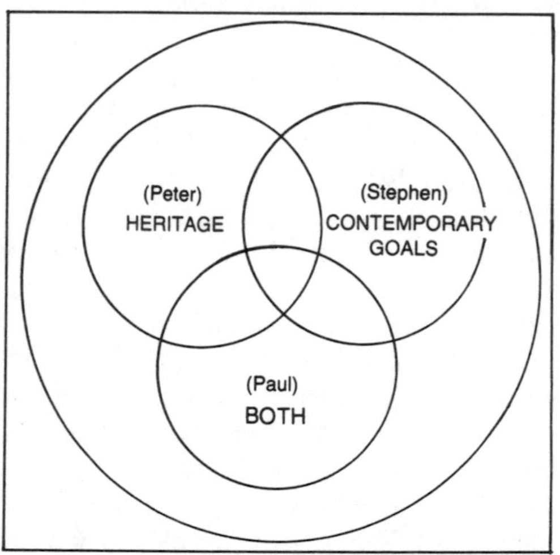

An Inside Look at Your Ministry Formation (fig. 4)

Peter represents the past heritage *from* which you are coming. Stephen puts you in touch with your present struggle to identify contemporary goals *through* which you are working. Paul illustrates the freedom of movement beyond your past heritage and your present struggle with a clear sense of direction that is oriented *to* the future. Your personal diagram may consist of some larger or smaller circles, but the forces of tradition, transition, and mission are all at work in your ministry formation for effective leadership. A comparison of your time line, your formation pattern, and your leadership style (see fig. 5) will help you to draw a more accurate picture of your current stage of professional development.

Time Line	Formation Pattern	Leadership Style
Past (Heritage Type)	Tradition (Coming *From*)	Priest (Empathetic Style)
Present (Contemporary Goals Type)	Transition (Working *Through*)	Prophet (Efficient Style)
Future (Bridging Type)	Mission (Going *To*)	Prophet, Priest, and King (Effective Style)

Reconstructing Your Own Ministry Formation (fig. 5)

If it is confusing to view the three parts of your formation process simultaneously, each column uses a different vocabulary to describe the same overlapping circles. Any difficulty you have in reconstructing your formation pattern may be explained in the next observation.

Second, Luke's master stories will help you to identify the dominant style of your pastoral leadership. You know intuitively to stop the scan on the story that fits you best. Are you struggling, like Peter, with the restraints of your pre-conditioning that inhibit your empathetic leadership?

Are you, like Stephen, exhibiting a bold display of efficient leadership in dealing with the obstacles to inclusive ministry in the present? Or are you, like Paul, charting new frontiers of effective cross-cultural leadership that promise to enrich your future?

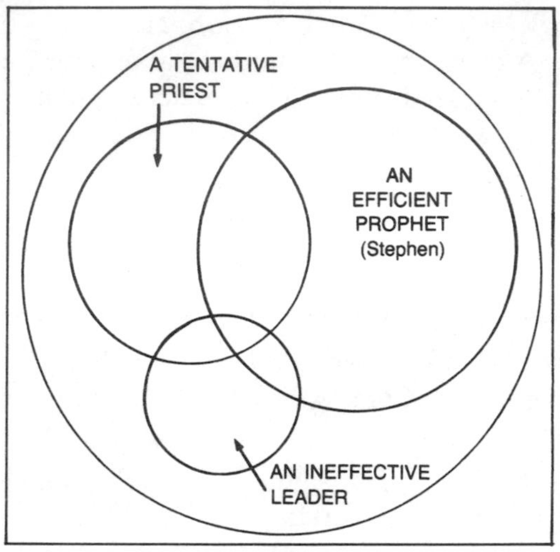

A Dominant Prophetic Style of Ministry Formation (fig. 6)

My pastoral leadership for the past twenty years has been developing primarily from a dominant efficient style to an experimental empathetic pattern. A previous attempt at documenting my story from 1965 to 1970, as a *Journey Toward Renewal,* described the beginning of the experience as a task oriented pattern. One observer viewed my journey as "a conceptualizing administrator who can quickly theorize a programmatic response to an articulated need." At the end of the five-year experiment in church renewal, I had discovered a person centered pattern. This growing awareness of empathy was described as movement "from object orientation ('renewal of the church or radical social change') to person centeredness ('renewal begins with me')."[26] In contrast to the previous performance demands of an efficient leadership style, my present course correction continues to utilize the personhood demands of an empathetic style. My own life story is a movement from the goal orientation of Stephen to the person centered style of Peter. The discipline of this study is pushing me toward the more balanced style of Paul.

My reflecting on the pattern of my ministry formation will help you to get a better picture of how your own diagram should be drawn. In 1965, my leadership style could be diagrammed as a one-sided prophet who was trying to become a priest (see fig. 6). In 1970, there was a definite shift to an enthusiastic priest who was willing to be less of a prophet (see fig. 7). Two experiences of clinical pastoral education contributed significantly to this course correction. For me, the turning point in my ministry formation was the recognition of a need for reworking the tradition from which I was coming. The experience of transition enabled me to begin again by working through the underdeveloped side of my empathetic leadership. My inner traits of "intuition-feeling" were shut up in a bottle that was sealed by the outer traits of "extroversion-judging."[27] Recognizing this outer cork as a hindrance to the true self that was concealed in the bottle followed. The less emphasis put on controlling the

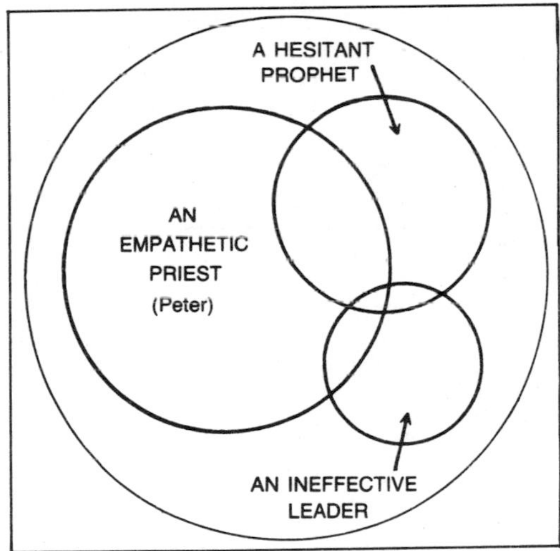

Dominant Priestly Style of Ministry Formation (fig. 7)

tightness of the cork, the more freedom and visibility came to my inner traits. The only way out of my bottled-up self was through releasing the pressure on the cork.

This early phase of my ministry formation was captured in the slogan of a Chicago counseling center: "The only way out is through." Transition became the unavoidable link that connected my incomplete tradition with my anticipated misson of pastoral leadership. A recent sabbatical leave was clearly an occasion for my continuing to develop the concealed priestly side of my ministry formation. Now, the goal of my formation is one of becoming a more balanced and effective leader, such as Paul, who can be a priest and/or a prophet as the occasion demands (see fig. 8).

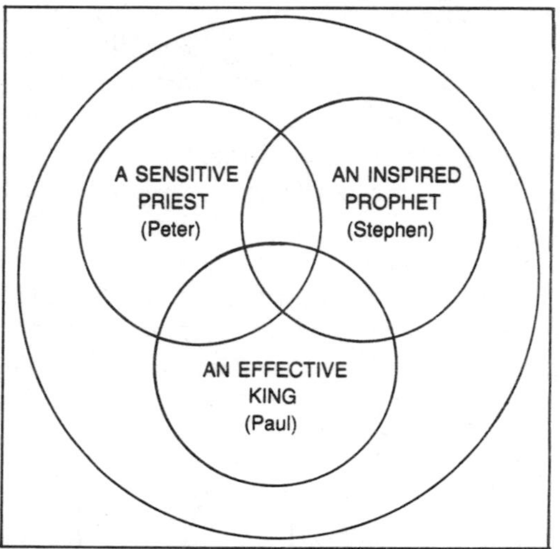

The Goal of Effective Leadership (fig. 8)

The interdependence of the qualities of prophet, priest, and king will continue to be the challenging part of my ministry formation in the future. My effectiveness as a church leader, like yours, depends on this kind of integration.

I hope you have identified your uniqueness in one or more of Luke's master stories. My story is intended as an encouragement for moving you beyond a purely efficient style of leadership. By itself, this style can be a problem, except in ministry situations that are mainly administrative or that require drastic action. Therefore, the remaining chapters will point you in the other two directions.

The empathetic leadership style of Peter will be illustrated by Pastor Betty Hochstetler of Chicago. Her contemporary story embodies *a crisis of pastoral authority* within a congregational context. Paul's effective style of leadership is exemplified by Augustine of Hippo. His historical narrative describes the processes by which *an identity crisis* is resolved during the first decade of ministry. Another example of Paul's effective style of leadership is Wayne E. Oates of Louisville. His contemporary story places *a crisis of faith* within the larger context of spiritual formation.

You now recognize the entry issues of pastoral authority, identity formation, and faith development that were identified in John Mark's story. They served the purpose of putting one item on the agenda of your ministry formation—*knowing your limitations*. Now, you have added another item to that agenda—*knowing your strengths*. The interplay of these two issues puts a spotlight on your present style of leadership and what you would like it to become during your first decade of ministry.

Since you are the person who is primarily responsible for your ministry formation, let's continue the exercise of theological and self-reflection. Both processes are essential to your growth as a Christian minister. The issue of identity formation calls for self-reflection. The issue of faith development requires theological reflection. The issue of authority is in the "crossover" category because it emerges from the other two and must be approached from the standpoint of theological and self-reflection.

Questions for Self-reflection

1. Are you able to identify "your characteristic manner of expressing your values and executing your work" (your style)? Is it tilted toward personhood values or performance goals?

personhood

2. How is your style expressed in pastoral leadership within a congregational context (or wherever God has called you to serve)? Is it primarily empathetic (person centered), efficient (program oriented), or effective (both or either as needed)?

3. How would you describe Peter as an empathetic leader? Can you work in depth with people who are as different as Jews and Gentiles?

4. How would you describe Stephen as an efficient leader? Can you specify situations in which this style is not only appropriate but also necessary?

5. Do you think that Paul started his ministry with the natural balance of an effective leader? How would John Mark answer that question?

6. Is it necessary to combine natural gifts with learned skills in order to become an effective leader? Was Paul by nature more goal oriented or person centered?

7. Can you identify your natural gift as working with people or as administering programs? What skills will you need to develop in order to become a more balanced, effective leader?

8. Do you have a senior colleague who can help you to recognize your uniqueness as a professional church leader? Would your personal reflection be enriched by the reality test of another perspective?

9. What is your goal for becoming a more effective leader? What traits have to change in order for your goal to be reached?

Questions for Theological Reflection

1. Are you more comfortable with the management terms mentioned above or with the biblical leadership types of prophet, priest, and king? Do you also have a grasp of your biblical leadership type?

2. Does your normal priestly role of leading in worship limit you to the maintenance mentality of a religious functionary? Are you

free, like Peter, to move beyond these restraints when the pastoral situation demands more flexibility?

3. Do you often get caught up in the prophetic role of a charismatic leader? Does your preaching/teaching, like Stephen, model a willingness to take risks and to go against the stream of popular religious thinking?

4. Are you moving toward an integration of the priestly and prophetic styles of leadership? Does your organizational ability, like Paul's, maintain a balance between the needs of people and the development of programs?

5. Do you consider the kingly office to be a religious or a political concept? What are some contemporary ways in which this office may be bestowed on a church leader?

6. Does your relationship with a senior colleague include the dimension of theological reflection? Are you both working harder at the theological or the psychological side of your ministry formation?

7. Can you draw a diagram that illustrates your current stage of ministry formation? What do you want the diagram to look like at the end of the first decade of your ministry?

8. Can you summarize the limitations and strengths that have characterized your ministry formation up to this point? What will have to change if you are going to reach the goal that is projected for your first decade of ministry?

9. What are the primary issues of theological reflection in your ministry? Are they connected with your identity, your faith, and/or your authority?

CHAPTER THREE

TESTING YOUR PASTORAL LEADERSHIP: *BETTY HOCHSTETLER*

In their playfulness, children often confuse the difference between reality and illusion. Working on the yard of our Glen Ellyn home is one of my regular responsibilities. Our two-year-old neighbor, Matthew, often watches me work outside. Once, a pile of sticks in the front yard was about ready for the garbage bag. I pointed down at the neatly gathered pile and said to Matthew, "What's that?" In his innocent way, he replied, "A castle." The reality of dirty sticks became, for him, the illusion of a beautiful castle.

Of course, there is a thin line between an illusion that is fantasy and a Dream that generates excitement and vitality for your professional development. Technically, the capitalization of the word *Dream* sets it apart from a night dream or a daydream. It becomes a vision or an imagined possibility of the goal for your development into an effective pastoral leader. Some testing is necessary to make sure that a young adult's Dream is not a fanciful illusion. The uniqueness of your style of leadership is one aspect of reality testing.

Perhaps your initial period of ministry has been complicated by a painful experience. Your present reality may be more a pile of sticks than the beautiful Dream for effective ministry toward which you are moving. Your ministerial experience may include the loss of a loved one, an unexpected conflict with another person, an experience of rejection for which you were not prepared, or a need to change your career direction because of a more realistic assessment of your gifts. Your harsh reality may appear, on the surface, to be an experience of failure and defeat—such as Stephen's inability to persuade his Jewish antagonists about the world mission of the Church.

You may also feel like a failure in terms of your inability to help your congregation move from tradition to mission. The story of Betty Hochstetler will help you to recognize transition in your ministry. Her traumatic experience will suggest that God is unrelentingly working out his purpose in the worst possible things that can happen to you.

Her story takes place within the context of a local congregation. This New Testament pattern first appeared as an informal home gathering or "house church" (Acts 12:12). The more formal organization that sent out the first missionary team was called "the church at Antioch" (Acts 13:1). Later, "they gathered the church together and reported what God had done" (Acts 14:27). The designation of official leaders, such as "elders" (Acts 20:17), "deacons" (I Timothy 3:8), and "pastors" (Ephesians 4:11), followed.

The challenge of serving a voluntary association of God's people, known as a local church, is illustrated by Pastor Betty's story. Her official title of "co-pastor" along with her husband, Lee, will not be as important as the natural gift she had for becoming a pastoral leader. The clarification of her style of leadership will enable you to enter into the same kind of self-examination.

This chapter will provide a reality test for determining whether you are naturally gifted as an empathetic or as an efficient leader. It will also suggest some biblical guidelines for using your pastoral leadership in a local congregation. Your movement toward an effective style of leadership will be tested further in terms of your awareness of inclusion dynamics and your compatibility with the type and size of the congregation you are serving.

PASTOR BETTY'S STORY OF EMPATHETIC LEADERSHIP

Some married couples respond to the call of God together and seek out a place of service that is open to a pastoral team.

Co-pastors Lee and Betty Hochstetler found this kind of opportunity in a small Mennonite congregation in Chicago in the fall of 1976. They had attended the Associated Mennonite Biblical Seminaries in Elkhart, Indiana, during the previous academic year and were looking forward to a year of practical experience. An eleven-month internship and related academic work was provided by the Seminary Consortium for Urban Pastoral Education (SCUPE). Their Midwestern seminary and four others had been invited to launch this program during the 1976–77 academic year by a small group of evangelical pastors in Chicago. Pastor Betty happened to be the member of the pastoral team who was available to tell me her story during a field visit in 1982.

Beginning with the Facts

The Grace Mennonite Church, on the southside of Chicago, was a struggling congregation of twenty-five senior adults in 1976 when the elderly pastor resigned. A young couple still in seminary assumed the full pastoral responsibilities. The church was able to broaden its ministry to include the community in which it was located. The loss of the old frame structure was followed by the construction of a new building. The completion of this brick structure in the fall of 1980 was actually the first new church building that had been constructed in Chicago in five years. The growing congregation of 150 regular attenders had gotten some help from the General Conference Mennonite Church in order to complete the project at a cost of $275,000.

However, the "facts" do not tell the whole story. The meaning of Pastor Betty's story goes back to an unexpected traumatic experience. The dedication of the new church building was actually the completion of a renewal process that had started six years earlier.

The Rest of the Story

The culture shock of moving from a small town in Indiana to a sprawling metropolitan area was compounded by the surprising news that the pastor of the Grace Mennonite Church had just resigned. The SCUPE intern assignment for Lee and Betty was adjusted to include the full pastoral responsibilities for this small-membership congregation. The twenty-five active members average sixty years of age. In addition to the regular worship services, the pastors were asked to work with a solitary Sunday school class of six elderly persons. The internship experience during the first year was largely a matter of survival. A maintenance ministry was complemented by ministry to the community, a requirement of the SCUPE program. Perhaps even more important was their decision to remain as co-pastors beyond the SCUPE intern year.

The original church building, a modest white frame structure, had an apartment on the second floor, which was used as a church office. A parsonage next to the church building provided a home base for the ministers in the changing blue-collar community. As might be expected, many opportunities for counseling with neighborhood residents became an important part of their daily routine, especially for Pastor Betty. For example, she befriended an abused homemaker who was being harassed by her common-law husband. Since this victim of domestic violence had nowhere else to go, Pastor Betty invited her to live "temporarily" at the parsonage in the spring of 1977. The police and a social worker would try to deal with the woman's husband. He took the situation into his own hands, however, as the co-pastors ended their first year of ministry. Because the angry man was denied contact with his wife, his resentment toward the co-pastors expressed itself in another form of violence. He threw a fire bomb into the old church building while the ministers were working upstairs in the office. Lee and Betty escaped, but the frame building was totally gutted.

The previous *status quo* routine was no longer an option in the crisis precipitated by the fire bombing. A survival mentality, rooted in the narrow confines of one ethnic tradition, had been shattered. The fire forced those who remembered their General Conference Mennonite Church heritage to reevaluate what it meant to be a struggling church in a changing community. Worship services were held in the old two-car garage that was renovated with the help of many neighborhood residents. It was soon packed to capacity with about sixty persons on Sunday morning. Then, the decision was made to rebuild a half-block north of the former church building. The broadening base of participation by local residents with no Mennonite background gradually shifted the character of the congregation to a community church; it became the Grace Community Church long before the name was changed. A new decentralized structure of support groups even attracted residents with no religious background. Eventually, an instrumental ensemble added a distinctive expression of joy to the "up-beat" services of worship in the new building. The newest program idea was the vision of starting a Holistic Health Care Center as a further outreach to the community.

Like the master stories of Luke, Pastor Betty's story of traumatic disruption became the transition that facilitated movement from tradition to mission. Her good deed, much like Stephen's harsh words, called forth a violent response. Fortunately, she lived through the crisis and learned from the experience.

> We've seen the church grow from a small building and a survival mentality to one that is moving, growing, and becoming a people that sees possibilities. We are God's people, and because we are, something is happening. The fire has been blessed, because it has pushed us to do something we wouldn't have done otherwise.[1]

A sure sense of pastoral authority is communicated in this theological reflection. The disastrous fire led to an unexpected blessing. God clearly used this transition experience to move a traditional congregation toward an intentional mission to the community in which it was located. Pastor Betty's story ends with an "unhindered" celebration of community ministry at the dedication service of the renamed Grace Community Church. Discernible movement from the *tradition* of the old Grace Mennonite Church, through the "old garage" phase of *transition,* led to the *mission* of the Grace Community Church. This leadership process became for co-pastors Lee and Betty "the story of [their] life."

The happy ending of this story need not obscure the reality of an empathetic style of leadership getting an inexperienced pastor into deep trouble. What if the estranged husband had chosen to fire-bomb the church during a worship service? But for the grace of God, someone could have been seriously injured in the fire. The way it actually happened, the loss of the church property was an economical disaster. The emotional loss of a sacred place to the remaining members was an even greater shock.

Pastor Betty was led by her feeling of empathy for a person caught in a domestic trap. It was natural for her to open her home as a refuge from the storm. Perhaps, she had not yet become aware of an appropriate shelter in which the battered woman could remain anonymously. Working with a social worker on this referral approach may have been another option. Pastor Betty could have chosen to maintain a supportive friendship during the period of crisis by following this more efficient style.

It is a credit to the heroic leadership of this pastoral team that the congregation survived at all. The growth from the "hand to mouth" financing of twenty-five persons in 1976 to an annual budget of $38,000 and 150 worshipers in 1980 is phenomenal. Behind the scenes, Betty is also a part-time student at McCormick Theological Seminary. The dedication of the new building in 1980 coincided with her receiving the M.Div. degree.

You will be interested in the next phase of Betty's professional development. The ministry of the pastoral team concluded in Chicago in 1985. Lee accepted a call to become pastor of the North Danvers Mennonite Church in Danvers, Illinois. Betty went with him, but chose to develop her empathetic style of leadership in a different direction. She decided to work toward her D.Min. degree in pastoral care and counseling through the Illinois Pastoral Services Institute in nearby Bloomington.

Having become aware of her natural empathetic gift, Betty was moving toward specialization in what she did best. The option of a Christian counseling ministry would enable her to be herself. A possible tension of competing with her husband in pastoral ministry also would be removed. A two-career pattern would make it possible for their ministries to complement each other. The former co-pastors were on their way to becoming separate professional persons.

By comparison, your initiation into pastoral ministry may seem rather tame. Would you have been an empathetic leader, like Pastor Betty, and opened your home to a person in need? Or would you have chosen the more efficient route of finding a shelter for the community resident? In either case, would you have had the courage to persist through the crisis period so that a tragedy could be turned into a triumph? The details of reality testing your style of leadership will be different; yet, you can be better prepared for whatever may happen by taking a closer look at three stages of the leadership process in the narrative framework of the book of Acts.

TESTING YOUR STYLE OF LEADERSHIP

In the previous chapter, you learned that Luke's master stories in the book of Acts represent formative events in the lives of three church leaders. Each story personifies a larger narrative section of Luke's unfolding drama of the early church:

Peter's formation overcomes the prevailing tradition. Stephen's confrontation begins the transition. Paul's transformation is the impetus for mission. Therefore, these three ministry prototypes, viewed together, suggest a basic principle of pastoral leadership that will give direction to your ministry formation during your first decade of Christian service. Pastoral leadership is not so much a particular goal to be attained as it is an ongoing process of exploration, which will enable you to *renegotiate the past*, to *engage the present*, and to *create the future*. From an individual perspective, this leadership process is illustrated by Peter's trance-vision, by Stephen's martyrdom, and by Paul's high calling. From a corporate perspective, an ongoing process of renewal became visible as the early Church moved from tradition, through transition, to mission.

A sense of movement is contained in the flow of Luke's master stories in relation to "coming from," "working through," and "going to." There is power in those prepositions. The three steps, translated into biblical guidelines for pastoral leadership, become diagnosis/envisioning, planning/spontaneity, and intentionality/action. You will recognize these biblical dynamics as leadership guidelines for church renewal in Pastor Betty's story. Grappling with tradition, as in Peter's story, was her initial experience as a co-pastor of the Grace Mennonite Church. Working through transition, as in Stephen's story, she emerged from the fire-bombing crisis that led to the "old garage" happening. The goal of mission, as in Paul's story, became the unhindered ministry of the Grace Community Church. Your grasp of these guidelines is more than theory. Your practice of ministry becomes the means of reality testing the style of leadership you choose to use in your ministry.

Diagnosis/Envisioning: Antidotes for Tradition

Tradition can be either a positive or a negative factor, but in either case it is an unavoidable reality in every congregation. It is positive if it represents conserving the best *tradition* (literally, enjoying "that which has been handed down") from the past. It may also be used to limit, to bind, to restrict, or to enslave in a form of bondage. The latter use is synonymous with the *status quo* (literally, the "state in which" anything is). Then it has the connotation of rigidity and inflexibility. Ralph Neighbour says with tongue in cheek that the seven last words of the church are: "We never tried it that way before."[2] Tradition may be understood more negatively than positively in a local congregation. In that situation, the challenge of pastoral leadership is to engage in a process of diagnosis and/or envisioning. The first approach requires a knowledge of your congregation as an institution based on a study of the past and the present. The second approach puts the emphasis on deciding as an institution in which direction you want to go in the future.

This tension is inherent in Acts 1:6-8. Luke suggests that the initial disciples were oriented toward diagnosis and that the risen Christ projected the alternative of envisioning. The disciples' question was, "Lord, are you at this time going to restore the kingdom to Israel?" (Acts 1:6). Their thoughts about the past and their immediate expectations for the present were a kind of diagnosis. They saw in Jesus the Jewish Messianic hope of a restored political rule on earth. The reply of the risen Christ, "You will be my witnesses" (Acts 1:8), is a form of envisioning. A spiritual rule on earth, in which the disciples would be able to participate, was now possible because of the anticipated empowerment of the Holy Spirit. The resurrected Christ did not diagnose the disciples' past and present understanding of a politically motivated Jewish Messiah. Instead, he presented them a future vision of what they could become in the power of the Holy Spirit.

In relation to the Grace Mennonite Church, the crisis of an unexpected fire removed the necessity for diagnosis. Fortunately, co-pastors Lee and Betty had a vision of what the congregation could become by witnessing to their immediate community. The most excitement in the interview with Pastor Betty was expressed in her description of the "happening" in the crowded garage. The ambiance of sixty people "stacked like sardines" was a contemporary version of what it must have been like in the upper room (Acts 1:12-14).

In the earlier setting, 120 had gathered on that celebrative Pentecost, when the empowerment of the Jerusalem church became a reality. Peter's powerful sermon was delivered on the occasion of the Jewish Pentecost in Jerusalem (Acts 2:14-36). As a result, many Jews and proselytes were added to the ranks of believing Christians. A diagnosis of that important event within the framework of Jewish cultural captivity (negative tradition) made the subsequent event in a crowded Roman household even more significant. Peter was also the preacher at the Gentile Pentecost in Caesarea (Acts 10:44-48). The envisioning of the risen Christ was fulfilled even more completely with the conversion of the God-fearing Gentile named Cornelius and his household.

In the context of your ministry, do you need to exercise pastoral leadership in the form of diagnosis and/or envisioning? Although the biblical narrative suggests a process from diagnosis to envisioning, an unexpected crisis may remove the need for diagnosis. Pastor Betty's story, like Stephen's sermon, jumps immediately to envisioning an expanded mission for the Church.

PLANNING/SPONTANEITY: CATALYSTS FOR TRANSITION

The ongoing process by which the early Church moves from tradition to mission becomes the pivotal Transition narrative. Yet, the impatience and impulsiveness of pastoral leadership often implies that this step does not exist at all. My disappointment as a young minister could have been predicated in attempting to organize an all-church visitation program. The announcement of this new program from the pulpit on Sunday morning was a response to my realization that more visitation by church members was one of the greatest needs of our inner city congregation in Trenton, New Jersey. When only one person showed up on Tuesday evening, my initial reaction was to blame the apparent apathy on a lack of Christian commitment. Now, a more realistic assessment would point a finger at the young minister who tried to launch the movement from tradition to mission without any thought of the preparatory stage of transition.

Lyle E. Schaller insists that "you can't get there [to mission] from here [tradition]." He describes the connecting transition experience as planning: "The planning effort should be focused on getting from here (the reality of today) to there (the vision of what God is calling Central Church to be and to be doing five years hence)."[3] This intentional approach to transition requires alert leadership, whether it is empathetic or efficient.

The biblical narrative, however, balances the planning effort of appointing the Seven (Acts 6:1-6) with the spontaneity of Stephen's "life after death" vision (Acts 7:55-60), of Paul's sudden encounter with the risen Christ (Acts 9:1-9), and of Peter's formative trance-vision (Acts 10:9-16). These master stories provide convincing evidence that God has a persistent way of breaking through and changing the best made plans of human ingenuity. As in Luke's master stories, Pastor Betty also learned that the starting point of transition may be a crisis experience. What you least expect to happen may be God's way of advancing his kingdom enterprise, if you find you are able to turn a problem into an opportunity.

Since the principle cannot be denied that "people own what they help to create," planning is important. Peter and John were sent from Jerusalem when it was learned that the people of Samaria were accepting God's message (Acts 8:14). Yet, Philip was guided by an angel of the Lord in order to be in the right place at the right time for making contact with the Ethiopian eunuch (Acts 8:26-27). Planning needs to be balanced with spontaneity. It must remain open to the unexpected surprises that may come to you. Reading Luke's historical narrative from this perspective, we discover three surprises.

1. Those who were sent (the apostles) were not the ones who went (Acts 1:8 and 8:1).
2. Those who finally went (unnamed persons from Cyprus and Cyrene) were not sent (Acts 11:19-21).
3. Those who were finally sent (Barnabas and Saul) had a dispute as they went (Acts 15:39-40).

The true test of pastoral leadership is your ability to respond creatively to unexpected crises by turning problems into opportunities.

You may not get everything you want in life. You may be denied a certain position because it is not part of your particular calling. Other disappointments may come your way because you need the experience of passing through "the valley of the shadow" as a resource for helping troubled persons. Do not underestimate the surprises God has for your ministry! The key to coping with surprises is openness to interpretation in the midst of a crisis. You may discover God's presence at the crossroads, when one path is closed and another is opened. John Mark came to that realization. You may discover God's presence in the midst of a great tragedy. When your ministry seems to be out of control, Lloyd J. Ogilvie's reflection on the persecution of Stephen's followers will give you another perspective.

> Historical honesty forces us to admit that this [scattering] was not point one in a carefully outlined strategy of the early Church for the expansion of the fellowship to the world. The followers of the resurrected Lord were equally amazed that their zeal for Christ superseded ancient prejudices. Without thinking about it, they shared the good news wherever they went.[4]

Roland Allen correctly described what happened as *The Spontaneous Expansion of the Church.*[5] Reflecting on and learning from God's surprises in your life and in the life of your congregation will provide appropriate transitional experiences for "getting from here to there."

INTENTIONALITY/ACTION: MANDATES FOR MISSION

The resource of tradition and the catalyst of transition lead to the advancement of mission. The ultimate goal of mission pushes pastoral leadership toward the third step of intentionality. Once you find the opportunity that is concealed in your problem, you can be even more intentional about drawing others into its implementation. The action step is one of organized initiative, which follows the biblical pattern of launching the world mission of the Church, beginning in Antioch (Acts 13:1-3).

The movement from Jerusalem to Antioch has been completed. The "Ya'll come" missionary strategy of the Jerusalem church is superseded by the "Let's get up and go" approach of the Antioch church. The delicate balance between positive tradition and propulsive mission calls for both *equipping,* like Jerusalem, and *sending,* like Antioch.

The ominous side of negative tradition, however, is dominant in the conclusion of the Mission narrative. Paul presented Jesus' claims in Rome "before the Gentiles and their kings and before the people of Israel" (Acts 9:15). In this way, Luke skillfully resolves the contrast between Jewish willful blindness and Gentile responsiveness (Acts 28:23-31). The self-exclusion of Jewish Christians who "would not believe" (Acts 28:24*b*) caused Paul to break off his final interview. He accepted the consolation prize (in Acts 28:28*b*) that "the Gentiles . . . will listen" (literally, "it is they who will hear"). The challenge of pastoral leadership is also to help your congregation "hear with their ears [and] understand with their hearts" (Acts 28:27*b*). The tragic consequence of preserving tradition as an end in itself must be rejected in favor of using it as a means to the end of equipping God's people for mission. The initial step of diagnosis/envisioning, with the help of surprises that energize planning with spontaneity, leads to the final step of sending God's people into mission by means of intentional action.

These guidelines become relevant for your pastoral leadership if Jerusalem is identified as "our kind of people."[6] Focusing on the ultimate goal of foreign missions or international ministries is much easier than dealing with other kinds of people in your own community. A closer examination of these transition dynamics will enable you to become aware of the movement from tradition to mission.

TESTING YOUR INCLUSION DYNAMICS

Pastor Betty's openness to an inclusive ministry with a community resident becomes a test case of what you would do in a similar situation. The way she moved so quickly from the well-established Mennonite tradition to inclusive mission resulted in making the situation literally explosive. The in-between phase of transition was missed. Her empathetic style of leadership leads her to take a "Lone Ranger" approach to the problem. It did not seem necessary to include the congregation in her decision to make the parsonage into a half-way house for a physically abused community resident. Would the church have approved of the use of the parsonage in this way, if asked for a policy decision? Would other alternatives have emerged if Pastor Betty had expressed her concern for this distressed person? A more judgmental congregation might have ended Pastor Betty's ministerial career as a result of the fire-bombing! Instead, a loving and compassionate attitude was demonstrated toward the persons whose actions innocently caused the disaster.

The lack of formal communication with the leadership core of the congregation can be traced to a fundamental difference in orienation. Lyle E. Schaller suggests that local congregations consist of four groups of people. In summary, these are:

> (1) Those with shared roots, or *heritage*, which are the basis for that person's strong loyalty or commitment to *this* congregation; (2) Those who feel a strong commitment or sense of loyalty to this congregation because of what it is doing in ministry now through contemporary goals; (3) A usually smaller group of members feel a sense of commitment to that parish through *both* heritage ties and contemporary goals; and (4) The members who do not fit into any category tend to be the ones who do not feel a strong sense of commitment to *this* parish now.[7]

The heritage orientation of the Mennonite congregation was initially very one-sided, except for the young co-pastors. They were interested in ministry now, through the contemporary goals of presence among and service to community residents. The elderly minister who had just retired may have been aware of this inevitable tension. The fire-bombing only dramatized the difference between the maintenance mind-set of the congregation and the mission mood of Pastor Betty.

The remarkable overcoming of this impasse can only be attributed to the bridging role of Pastor Lee.[8] His quiet support was felt among the heritage types *and* the newcomers from the neighborhood, who were gradually assimilated into the congregation. The abused homemaker was among the first of many community residents who chose to affiliate with the "old-timers." Only a few occasional visitors fit the fourth spectator grouping.

A comparison of the three primary groups in the Grace Mennonite Church with the threefold biblical approach to pastoral leadership will be useful.

Biblical Leadership Pattern	Biblical Leadership Options	Schaller's Congregational Groupings
Tradition	Diagnosis/ * Envisioning	Heritage Type
Transition	Planning/ * Spontaneity	Contemporary Goals Type
Mission	* Intentionality/ * Action	Bridging Type

A Comparison of Biblical and Congregational Categories (fig. 9)

The asterisks above designate the leadership options that the co-pastors utilized during the four years leading up to the dedication of the Grace Community Church. Both the idealism of youth and the focus of the SCUPE program pushed them to begin their pastoral ministry with envisioning. The congregation also came to realize that the only hope for growth was to move beyond the tradition of their own Mennonite heritage. Yet, that vision for the future was "easier said than done." The spontaneity of Pastor Betty's empathetic leadership provided the "spark" that ignited the unexpected transition process. The movement toward mission was facilitated by the bridging role of Pastor Lee.

The heritage of this Mennonite congregation is reminiscent of the Hebrew orientation of the Jerusalem church (Acts 6:1). A similar community ministry was that with the Greek-speaking widows, which called forth the appointment of the Seven from the Hellenists (Acts 6:1-3). The Twelve (also called apostles) were the original heritage types; the Seven (not yet called deacons) were committed to contemporary goals. These two groups were represented by Peter and Stephen. Yet, it is the bridging role of Paul that blazed the trail of mission. He brought together the best of both worlds. As the occasion demanded, he could claim to be a Pharisee (Acts 23:6; 26:5; Philippians 3:5) or a Roman citizen (Acts 25:3-11).

The movement from tradition to mission includes a recognition of the invisible walls of exclusion and an intentional commitment to inclusion. Both pastors of the Grace Mennonite Church were trained in the art of assimilation. They knew that persons begin to feel that they belong when they are given a job or become part of a group. Newcomers with musical talent became involved with the jazz ensemble that played during the worship services. Others were invited to open their homes for Bible study groups in the community. Lyle E. Schaller describes what was happening in terms of four inclusion strategies:

> The individuals who become part of a group . . . *before* formally uniting with that congregation [are already being assimilated as a Type A group]. . . .
>
> [Those who] become members of a group, where membership in that group is meaningful, *after* uniting with that congregation [will be assimilated as a Type B group]. . . .
>
> Other new adult members are assimilated by accepting a *role* or office which gives them a sense of belonging and causes them to identify with the congregation. . . .
>
> A fourth route that some new members take which helps them feel assimilated is to accept a *task* or job as a worker.[9]

Reference has been made to the choice of the third strategy by the Jerusalem church. A new role, or office, was identified by appointing "seven men from among you who are known to be full of the Spirit and wisdom" (Acts 6:3).

The rapid growth of the Grace Mennonite Church after the fire can be attributed in part to the careful attention that was given to assimilating community residents. Like the Jerusalem church, it started with the conferring of a specific role or office on some of the newcomers. Two of Lyle Schaller's diagrams[10] will be combined in order to present the three overlapping groups in the Jerusalem church and its initial strategy of inclusion (see fig. 10). An inventory can be taken of the particular strategies of inclusion that are being used in your congregation.

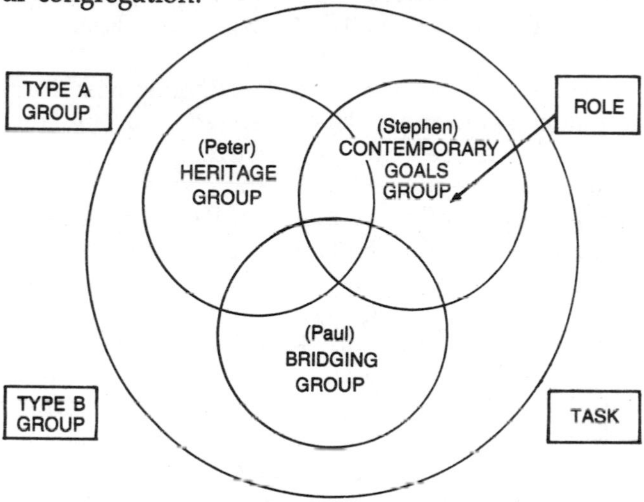

Biblical Dynamics of Inclusion (fig. 10)

The boxes outside the large circle suggest four ways in which ethnic, cultural, racial, or religious boundaries may be crossed. The four circles represent invisible walls surrounding the entire congregation and particular groups within it. The symmetry of the inner circles in the biblical model is, of course, too neat. You will want to draw a picture of your congregation that represents more precisely the size of the three inner groupings. You can put organizational names on the groups that are already in existence (Type A) or that need to be formed (Type B). You may choose to go directly to assigning a task or a job. The more formal procedure of working through channels to designate particular roles or offices will also be useful.

An examination of the inner dynamics of the congregation and how newcomers can be assimilated will be followed by a closer look at the type and the size of your congregation. There is a relationship between the style of leadership and the type and size of the congregation you hope to serve or are serving.

TESTING THE TYPE AND THE SIZE OF YOUR CONGREGATION

You have compared your style of leadership with the more distant ministry models of Peter, Stephen, and Paul. Yet, the biblical narratives are merely suggestive of Peter's empathetic style, Stephen's efficient style, and Paul's effective style. The contemporary ministry model of Pastor Betty is clearly empathetic and includes a major emphasis on pastoral care and counseling. Like Peter, she crossed over the boundaries of social custom. Inviting a community resident into her home for an extended period of time was beyond the call of duty. Her feeling of empathy for a hurting person set in motion the events that led to the threefold movement *from* the Grace Mennonite Church, *through* the devastating fire, *to* the Grace Community Church. Her sensitive nature seemed to outweigh her sensible objectivity in this case.[11] Inconvenience and the loss of privacy were put aside in favor of extending hospitality to "one of the least of these [sisters] of mine" (Matthew 25:40). Her more recent decision to do graduate study in pastoral care and counseling further confirms her empathetic orientation.

If you identify with her style of leadership, then you enjoy being with people and are stimulated by the variety of challenges that various people bring to you. You are able to establish and maintain long-term relationships that are perceived as therapeutic. You are concerned about the group life of your congregation (or other ministry context) and enjoy enabling other persons to become more expressive in group situations. Your empathy is most obvious if you engage in pastoral visitation on a regular basis. Meeting with people in their homes or work settings makes pastoral "calling" an essential supplement to the routine contacts before and after public worship services.

You should know by now whether you are an empathetic leader, such as the apostle Peter or Betty Hochstetler. But what does your style of leadership have to do with the type and size of your congregation? Is it just a mere coincidence that Pastor Betty seems to fit quite naturally into the life of a small membership congregation? Or does she have a natural people orientation that is valued more highly in this particular context? What may have begun as a fortunate coincidence is confirmed by the degree of investment Pastor Betty made in the people. Her pastoral sensitivity caused her to be sought out by those who had problems, whether in the congregation or in the community. It is significant that her experience of counseling an estranged homemaker took place in the early stage of the Grace Mennonite Church, when it was still a congregation of fewer than fifty persons. By the time of its dedication service, three years later, Grace Community Church had about 150 active persons. Pastor Betty's style of leadership was obviously better suited to the interpersonal demands of the smaller congregation than to the administrative demands of the larger congregation.

The intriguing thesis of Arlin J. Rothauge[12] suggests that there is a correlation between the type and the size of a congregation and style of leadership (see fig. 11).

With the help of this correlation, you have a rationale for checking the type and the size of your congregation and its leadership requirement. Pastor Betty embodied the chaplain function and certainly had the capacity for the trust building function. She would be less comfortable with the delegating role for which Pastor Lee was ideally suited. What started as a family church had become a pastoral church. Pastor Betty did not make the transition to the trust building function,

Type and Size of Congregaton	Leadership Requirement
A FAMILY CHURCH of 0-50 active members	Chaplain Function
A PASTORAL CHURCH of 50-150 active members	Trust Building Function
A PROGRAM CHURCH of 150-350 active members	Delegating Function

A Comparison of Congregational and Leadership Dynamics (fig. 11)

required by the larger congregation, as easily as did her husband. Her change of direction to a career in Christian counseling gave her the freedom to stay within the dynamics of the family church.

A comparison of the type and the size of your congregation with the expected leadership requirements provides a basis for a correlation to Luke's master stories and their contemporary expression in pastoral skills (see fig. 12).

Biblical Leadership Models	Expected Leadership Requirements	Preferred Pastoral Skill
PETER: The Empathetic Leader	Chaplain Function	Pastoral Care and Counseling
PAUL: The Effective Leader	Trust Building Function as the central pastor	Preaching and Teaching
STEPHEN: The Efficient Leader	Delegating Function as an executive	Church Administration

A Comparison of Biblical and Congregational Dynamics (fig. 12)

The ease with which Pastor Betty assumed the chaplain function, like Peter, is congruent with her desire for further development of her skills in pastoral care and counseling. The style of Pastor Lee's leadership, like Paul's, has the capacity of moving in either direction according to the circumstances. (The goal oriented style of Stephen is usually not an option by itself, since there are very few positions in Christian ministry that are mainly administrative.)

Does your natural gift for leadership fit the situation in which you have been called to serve? If you are serving a congregation that is not compatible with your natural style of leadership, you will want to give attention to the preferred pastoral skill that is required by your ministry context. The comparisons suggested above provide a basis for taking an inventory of your natural gift of leadership or needed skill development in relation to the type and the size of the congregation that you hope to serve or are presently serving. Learning to distinguish between which part of your style of leadership that is natural and which needs to be developed is a major step toward testing your pastoral effectiveness.

Pastor Betty's story of pastoral leadership touches your story in terms of availability mingled with vulnerability. It provides a contemporary window for identifying your style of leadership. Your dominant preference for leadership, like your personality preferences, is likely either empathetic or efficient. My efficient starting point is in contrast to Pastor Betty's empathetic beginning. Either style has some advantages in particular ministry contexts. The challenge of your ministry formation, however, is an intentional movement to a more balanced and effective integrated style. The remaining stories will open additional windows for viewing this integrative task of becoming an effective leader.

George G. Hunter III affirms the structure of the local congregation as God's primary vehicle for carrying out his mission in the world.[13] In an address given to an Advanced Church Growth Seminar in Pasadena in 1983, he concluded with a theological reflection: "The Church Growth movement has strengthened many churches, but its greatest contribution has been the unexpected by-product of helping ministers to reclaim their pastoral authority." Likewise, ministry formation will help you to become a more effective leader in a local congregation. But the exercise of your natural gift for leadership must emerge from a growing sense of pastoral authority.

Your internal authority is the God-given integration of identity formation and faith development. These aspects of your being may be perceived as limitations in the early stages of your ministry formation. They are targeted by the questions aimed at helping you to engage in theological reflection and in self-reflection.

Your external authority, which becomes visible through doing, is observed as your style of leadership. A tentative internal authority is perceived as a lack of confidence in exercising pastoral leadership. But a strong sense of inner well-being finds natural expression in an initial preference for either empathetic or efficient leadership.

Pastor Betty's story is the epitome of pastoral authority, which is expressed in an empathetic style of leadership. From the standpoint of self-reflection, the traumatic experience of "open house" taught her to go with the flow of her natural gift. Theological reflection helped her to reinterpret the devastating fire as a blessing in relation to her career development and in terms of church renewal. When the move to North Danvers, Illinois, was being negotiated, she decided to withdraw from even being considered as a co-pastor. Her change of direction to pastoral care and counseling is reminiscent of John Mark's withdrawal from a fast-moving missionary career for which he was not naturally gifted. Hindsight suggests that he may have been just as unsuited for the efficient demands of Paul as Pastor Betty was for the administrative demands of a larger congregation.

Not everyone is suited to the generalistic demands of pastoral ministry. An effective balance between empathy and efficiency is not automatic. Augustine's story will present a detailed description of a growing person who successfully rises to this challenge. You will be better prepared for the next step of integrating personhood and performance by reflecting on the questions below.

Questions for Self-reflection

1. Can you relate an experience in your ministry in which your empathetic leadership was recognized and appreciated? Is your natural style of leadership one of working with people in depth or on the surface?

2. Can you recall a particular situation in which you needed to exercise efficient leadership? Is your natural style of leadership indicated by referring often to successful statistics?

3. Is it your normal inclination to lead by using a process orientation or a goal orientation? Is there a connection between sensitivity in working with people and openness to a process orientation?

4. Are you dealing with only your personal perception of your style of leadership? Are there particular persons or testing instruments that would provide a second or third opinion?

5. Do the type and the size of your congregation correspond to your natural gift as a pastoral leader? If not, what preferred skill will be expected in order to meet the demands of your particular congregation?

Questions for Theological Reflection

1. Can you illustrate, from your life story, the difference between a Dream that is achievable and an illusion that is pure fantasy? Can you examine your present career goal in ministry from this perspective?

2. What is the most traumatic experience you have had in ministry? Have you subjected that event to the interpretation of theological reflection?

3. Does that event add any further confirmation of your natural preference for exercising pastoral leadership? Do the stages of tradition, transition, and mission provide any help in understanding that event?

4. Would a further response to this difficult situation suggest the

need for diagnosis (a better understanding of the past) or envisioning (an imaginative goal for the future)?

5. Was your initial response to the problem an act of spontaneity (doing what comes naturally) or a more deliberate effort of planning (profitting from the combined wisdom of many perspectives)?

6. Has this individual, or corporate, response led to more intentionality (purposeful direction of the mind) or specific action (definite decision of the will)?

7. Are you only comfortable working with persons like yourself, or does your leadership include a cross-cultural dimension? Does your own life-style encourage exclusion or inclusion of other ethnic and racial groups?

CHAPTER FOUR

INTEGRATING YOUR PASTORAL IDENTITY: *AUGUSTINE*

JUMPING IMMEDIATELY FROM THE NEW TESTAMENT PERIOD of the first century to the late twentieth century is quite common. However, considerable discernment is needed in order to make contact with a key church leader of the late fifth century. For me, the connection was made at the Metropolitan Opera during a performance of Berlioz's *Les Troyens.* It was my good fortune, as it turned out, not to be there on the official opening night of the centennial season but on the "real opening" on October 12, 1983. On that evening, the American soprano Jessye Norman sang the demanding role of Dido, Queen of Carthage, for the first time. Her previous performances as the prophetess Cassandra had been hailed as a bench-mark of modern operatic history. The longer role of Dido was an even greater sensation. The tragic conclusion of this monumental opera came when Aeneas decided to leave Carthage for Italy in order to become the founder of the Roman Empire. The pain of rejection, which Norman portrayed in Dido's death scene, is the rage of a broken heart. The proud, but distraught, African queen stabbed herself so that her body could be burned on a funeral pyre as her Trojan lover sailed away toward Italy. Jessye Norman's larger-than-life portrayal of Dido's death embodied the spirit of classical tragedy.

The triumph of that performance provided me with a point of contact with the life of Augustine. The same scene had once brought the youthful Augustine to tears. His weeping over Dido's death is mentioned in the most widely known of all his writings, the *Confessions* (I, 20-21).[1] Of course, his study of Latin included Virgil's *Aeneid*, which draws on Homer's Greek epics the *Illiad* and the *Odyssey*. The identification of the youthful Augustine, perhaps at an unconscious level, with the hero Aeneas is the beginning of the *Confessions*. It is hardly coincidental that he decided to write his autobiography as a spiritual odyssey of the soul.

Your impression of Augustine of Hippo (A.D. 354–430) is probably one of awe and admiration. You may remember this North African bishop as one of the greatest theologians in the history of Western Christendom. This Numidian church leader, who is also known as Saint Augustine, despite the greatness attributed to him in later years, was primarily a parish priest who became a prolific writer while serving as the "executive minister" of a program church. In his formative years, he began as an ordinary university student who was trying to find a direction for his life. Fortunately, the *Confessions* explores the inner world of his search for identity so that all can see the steps leading to his Christian conversion and his call to the ministry. This seminal work is the first Christian autobiography in which one whole person emerges from the interaction of mind, soul, and will.

In contrast to the previous ministry models of Peter and Stephen, Augustine is clearly a leader who does not limit his options. Like Paul, he became a minister for whom life was a unified whole. Like Kierkegaard in the nineteenth century, Augustine's theology emerged from this unified personhood and was shaped by his ongoing performance in ministry.

A few biographical details will help you to place Augustine within the context of his North African culture. He was born at Thagaste in A.D. 354 to an aspiring lower middle-class family. His father, Patricius, and his mother, Monica, sacrificed in order to give him the kind of liberal education that might lead him into an honored position in Roman society. His mother's wish that he enter the Christian ministry was a major influence on his life. Completing his formal education at the University of Carthage, he became a teacher of rhetoric. After a disappointing year of teaching in Rome, he received an important post in 384 as a public orator in Milan. Contact with the popular Bishop Ambrose in Milan was the catalyst that led to his conversion there in 386. Two years later, he returned to North Africa and established an informal monastic community in his home town. His call to the ministry followed in 391, when he was persuaded to enter the priesthood while visiting the aged Bishop Valerius in Hippo. Five years later, when Valerius died, Augustine became and remained bishop of Hippo until his death. The major portion of his literary career fell into the period of his bishopric (396–454). Among the first writings at the beginning of his strenuous administration as bishop of Hippo is the *Confessions* (397–400). It is an intensely personal work that carried his soul across the sea to the friends that he missed in Italy and elsewhere.

The life of Augustine is not easily penetrated; yet, the manageable framework of the *Confessions* provides a vivid picture of a young man whose search for meaning in life leads him to an integrated pastoral identity. As a fourth-century student of both philosophy and Scripture, Augustine is confronted by the war between Greek and Hebrew influences. Reading the *Confessions* will enable you to experience the loosening of the grip of Neoplatonic philosophy and the emergence of Christian theology and the pre-scientific understanding of the psychology of religion.

This chapter will enable you to explore several facets of Augustine's search for pastoral identity. The movement through four self-images will provide you with a basis for examining the steps leading to Augustine's conversion and his threefold integration of pastoral identity. The vocabulary will be different, but the struggle will be similar to yours. The capacity for personal introspection, which is evident in the *Confessions*, will present to you a challenge concerning the need for more intentional theological and self-reflection. Now, you are ready to take an imaginary journey with me to the North Africa of the late fifth century.

AUGUSTINE'S STORY OF IDENTITY FORMATION

The whole of the *Confessions* is a storehouse of information that can be approached from many directions. One of the most popular books ever written in Latin, this work has been a theological best seller for almost sixteen hundred years. Let me focus your attention on this literary classic by appropriating the portion of Augustine's story that deals with the formation of his personal identity. The telling of his story includes a movement through four self-images: a care-free student who is a sensual materialist, a public orator who is a professional rhetorician, a new Christian who dedicates his life to becoming a monastic scholar, and a maturing Christian who serves the Church as a pastoral leader.

Sensual Materialist (354–385)

Augustine's youthful interest in material possessions was intensified by an inordinate desire for sexual pleasure. He was a part of the dominant culture of Roman Africa, in which class differences were stratified quite rigidly. The common tendency was to seek an escape in sensual pleasure and material attachments. Augustine's first exposure to this narcissistic self-image was presumably through his father, Patricius (IX, 19-22). The emotional distance between father and son was in sharp contrast to the intense emotional attachment between Augustine and his mother, Monica, which lasted throughout his entire life.

A more dramatic exponent of this libertine life-style was his close friend, Alypius, a fellow student who arrived with him at the University of Carthage in 371. Alypius struggled to free himself from the attraction and domination of pagan shows (VI, 11-13). Augustine and Alypius were terrorized by the "old hands" in the *Eversores* fraternity (literally, society of "overturners" or "upsetters" [III, 6; V, 14]). These boistrous students were also sensual materialists. Augustine gave into this dominant mood by enjoying the Roman theater (IV, 1). He also succumbed to sensual pleasure by taking two mistresses (VIII, 2).

Augustine's primary intellectual stimulation during this student period came from the teachings of the Manichean sect and the philosophy of Neoplatonism. His disillusionment with the Manichean teacher Faustus caused him to break with this dualistic belief that the Church had classified as a Gnostic heresy (III, 10; V, 10-12). He held onto Plotinus' Neoplatonic philosophy, which eventually was "Christianized" during the course of his writing the *Confessions* (VII, 13; XI, 17; XIII, 2).

Public Rhetorician (376–386)

The highly respected role of the orator was supposed to contribute to upward social mobility in Roman society. It customarily opened up opportunities for fame, wealth, government appointment, and a successful life. This attainment provided Augustine a way of overcoming the rigidity of social class, as his social status climbed upward while excelling in the school of rhetoric in Carthage. His appointment as a teacher of rhetoric for a year in Rome began in 383 (III, 6: V, 22). The abuse of irresponsible students in Rome caused him to find a more satisfying career as professor of rhetoric in Milan from 384–386 (V, 24-25; VI, 3-4).

His new position of public orator brought him into contact with Ambrose, the venerable bishop of Milan, who became his Christian mentor and pastoral model. The rhetorical skill of Ambrose as a distinguished preacher was the attraction that initially drew Augustine to Christianity (V, 24-25; VI, 3-4). You will appreciate Augustine's skill even more because of the strong influence of his rhetorical training on the literary structure of the *Confessions*. The subtle unity of the *Confessions* can be detected on the basis of Augustine's rhetorical skill.[2] A summary of this perspective will enable you to see a professor of rhetoric at work. Augustine's sophistication prohibited him from explicitly disclosing how the various parts of the work fit together.

The theme of the "wandering of the soul" (*peregrinatio animae*) is the concept that implicitly brings the three parts of the work together into a unified whole. The autobiographical section (books I–IX) is the Neoplatonic story of the fall and return of the soul, which draws on his understanding of Plotinus. A play on the word *peregrinatio* provides the key to this section, which begins as a "wandering" away from God in books I to VII and ends with the "pilgrimage" toward God in books VIII and IX. The connotation of this word shifts according to the movement of the soul away from or toward God. Our author is, indeed, a professional rhetorician.

The second section, which is a philosophical meditation on memory (book X), describes Augustine's experience in the process of actually writing his historical narrative. The journey of the soul is first presented, then remembered, and finally grounded.

The third section (books XI–XIII) presents the creation story of Genesis 1:1–2:2 as the biblical foundation for the journey of his soul. The odyssey image, which Homer and Vergil had made commonplace for "wandering soul" in the ancient world, is fulfilled in the paradise of eternal "rest" in God (Genesis 2:2). Undoubtedly, Augustine's rhetorical skill is at work in the structure of the *Confessions*. Yet, he leaves the reader free to make the necessary connections between the seemingly separate parts of the work.

Monastic Scholar (386–400)

Augustine recognized God's providential guidance in holding up before him the ideal pastoral model of the Milanese Bishop Ambrose (V, 23). The turning point of his life was the garden experience of his conversion in 386 in Milan, when a voice as of a child said to Augustine: "Take up and read. Take up and read" (VIII, 29). His spontaneous reading of Paul's admonition in Romans 13:13-14 was interpreted as God's command to him to turn away from his former pursuits of sensual pleasure and public rhetoric to a life of Christian contemplation. More specifically, he understood the voice as a call to monastic life, which would provide a supportive environment for his emerging Christian identity.

Shortly after the garden experience in Milan, chest pains

affected Augustine's voice. His uncertain health suggested the need for an extended retreat from his teaching duties during the spring vacation. His break with the past was confirmed by his submitting a resignation as professor of rhetoric in Milan (IX, 7 and 13). By going with his mother and a group of friends to Cassiciacum, he created his own informal monastic community in a country villa near Lake Como (about fifty miles north of Milan near the Alps). Despite his illness, he combined lively dialogue with extensive literary work. The contentment of his new monastic life was expressed in the change of direction from the outward heat of the African sun to the inner warmth of a soul in the will of God (IX, 10). The modeling of Augustine's life of devotion and scholarship began to have an effect on his faithful companion, Alypius, and on the other catechumens.

The public confession of his interrelated conversion experience and monastic commitment was signified in the act of believer's baptism in Milan in 387. The autobiographical section of the *Confessions* ends with the death of his mother, Monica, at the Roman port of Ostia in 387. The *Confessions,* written approximately ten years after her death, is a fitting tribute to Monica, and it is evidence of his continuing grief. The longest and most touching narrative treatise relives his mother's life prior to her death (IX, 17-37). Her lifelong desire was that he become a follower of Christ and a catechumen of the Church. That wish was fulfilled, in part, by his conversion and even more by his writing of the *Confessions.*

Pastoral Leader (387–400)

The self-image of pastoral leader was on the horizon as the curtain dropped on the *Confessions* in 387. It was manifested clearly by the time he finished writing his autobiography thirteen years later. A recent biography presents the gradual process by which Augustine's monastic ideal merged with his pastoral role of bishop.[3]

The loss of his mother was followed by an extension of his stay in Rome for another year. Returning by ship to Carthage in 388, he stayed in his home town of Thagaste for the next two years and reestablished the cultural bonds of his African heritage; North Africa continued to provide the unbroken context for the rest of his productive life until his death forty-two years later. Having survived the strain caused by the intellectual centers of Rome and Milan, he would never again be a stranger from the southern provinces of the Roman Empire.

The two years spent in Thagaste allowed him to express his contemplative self-image by creating another informal monastic community, called "Servants of God." This little group of devoted friends, including Alypius, settled on Augustine's portion of the family estate. By the spring of 391, his inner transformation was secure enough to lead him along the high road from the hills down to the ancient seaport of Hippo. The aged Bishop Valerius was in urgent need of help and compelled Augustine to be ordained as a priest. In 393, the confidence that Valerius had in his younger colleague was expressed by his getting permission for Augustine's consecration as co-adjutor. This step ensured Augustine's succession as the next bishop of Hippo.

During these formative years in Hippo, Augustine was never alone. He recruited past friends to join him in the "Monastery in the Garden." There, his life of contemplation and study was combined with the manual labor of sowing seeds and tilling the soil. This *monasterium* became a seminary in the literal sense of the word—a "seed bed" from which Augustine's protégés were "planted out" as bishops in the leading towns of Numidia.[4] When Valerius died in 396, the new bishop of Hippo began his official duties as a pastoral leader. A coterie of trusted friends assisted him in implementing a dramatic revolution in the history of African Christianity.

By the time Augustine began writing the *Confessions* in 397, his Christian identity merged with his pastoral identity. This crucial period of his identity formation took place during ten years and in three settings:

1. Informally, at the villa of Cassiciacum in northern Italy during the spring vacation, immediately after his conversion in 386;

2. Informally, among "Servants of God" at Thagaste for two years after his return to North Africa in 388; and

3. Formally, with his colleagues at the "Monastery in the Garden" in Hippo for seven years, beginning in 391.

Before and after assuming the full administrative and pastoral responsibilities of bishop in 396, his close-knit community life provided continuous support for the exercise of pastoral leadership. Cardinal Bernadin, archbishop of Chicago, an ardent disciple of Augustine, describes the broad range of his mentor's concern as the diverse duties of "the chief pastor, an overseer of souls, the father in God of the whole community, Catholics, heretics, schismatics, and pagans."[5] Augustine can be understoood only as the whole person whose public ministry as a church official continued to be renewed by his consistent monastic life. It included prayer, meditation, study, and writing. The integration of contemplation, community, and scholarship was firmly established during his formative years as catechumen, priest, and co-adjutor. The self-image of pastoral leader was thoroughly formed during this preparatory period, which set the course for his life's work as the bishop of Hippo.

Augustine's identity formation was complete by the time he finished writing the *Confessions*. The four stages through which his self-image moved may help to interpret your search for an authentic identity. His story becomes a model for the person whose Christian calling begins inwardly and then receives external confirmation in ministry. It may be viewed as a case study of H. Richard Niebuhr's fourfold progression of Christian calling:

1. *The call to be a Christian*, which is variously described as the call to discipleship of Jesus Christ, to hearing and doing of the Word of God, to repetance and faith, etc.;

2. *The secret call*, namely, that inner persuasion or experience whereby a person feels himself directly summoned or invited by God to take up the work of the ministry;

3. *The providential call,* which is that invitation and command to assume the work of the ministry which comes through the equipment of a person with the talents necessary for the exercise of the office and through the divine guidance of his life by all its circumstances;

4. *The ecclesiastical call,* that is, the summons and invitation extended to a man by some community or institution of the Church to engage in the work of the ministry.[6]

Ministry is impossible from a Christian perspective apart from a personal encounter with God through Jesus Christ! For Augustine, the call to be a Christian and the secret call to a contemplative life occurred simultaneously. The providential call was experienced in Hippo when the recognition of his pastoral gifts led to his being pressured into service as a priest. The ecclesiastical call found expression in his consecration as bishop of Hippo. As Augustine's guidance of his close companion, Alypius, suggests, the self-image of pastoral leader included the developmental process of assisting colleagues with their ministry formation. Augustine's approach to ministry formation was rooted in a commitment to Christian community. This important part of his value system was a reaffirmation of the "common life" *(koinōnia)* of the early Church (Acts 2:44; 4:32).

In contrast to Augustine, your ministry experience may be characterized by the conspicuous absence of supportive community. The finding of your Cassiciacum villa, along with your colleagues, will enrich your ministry with mutual encouragement and accountability. The delicate balance between Augustine's investment in supportive community and the unending demands placed on him as a pastoral leader needs to be taken seriously. Your ministry formation will be greatly enhanced by the organizing of a pastoral support group, either on an informal basis or with the help of denominational leaders.[7]

If you are catching the spirit of Augustine, you will not want to be a "loner" in ministry. Friends and colleagues can help you to negotiate the entry issues that all ministers have to face. A closer look at Augustine's conversion and the resulting integration of his pastoral identity will remind you that ministry formation is inseparable from a commitment to Christian community.

THE TURNING POINT OF CHRISTIAN CALLING

Your reading of the *Confessions* will be easier if a few of the life stories that contributed to Augustine's ministry formation are presented in summary form. Three events became parables of his emerging pastoral identity: (1) the pear-stealing episode illustrates his initial self-image of sensual materialism; (2) the death of a dear friend opens up his sensitivity during the period of his public oratory; and (3) the garden experience of his personal transformation sets in motion his new Christian identity of monastic scholar/pastoral leader.

In contrast to the biblical narratives that are told in the third person, the *Confessions* is one long extended prayer in which Augustine tells his story to God. In a first-person conversation with God, he tells his story without fear that it will be judged trivial or unimportant. Telling your story in the atmosphere of prayer suggests that it is a matter of theological reflection and, you hope, self-reflection. Those matters that seem most insignificant come to the surface and are expressed in your time of meditation and prayer. Such was the case with the two life stories that prepared the way for Augustine's conversion. These experiences became the seed bed for his calling to the Christian ministry.

The discipline of recording his extended conversation with God brought to his mind the trivial adolescent experience of stealing pears.

> In a garden nearby to our vineyard there was a pear tree, loaded with fruit that was desirable neither in appearance nor in taste. Late one night—to which hour, according to our pestilential custom, we had kept up our street games—a group of very bad youngsters set out to shake down and rob this tree. We took great loads of fruit from it, not for our own eating, but rather to throw it to the pigs; even if we did eat a little of it, we did this to do what pleased us for the reason that it was forbidden. (II, 4)

Recent studies of the *Confessions* shift the emphasis of Augustine's struggle from guilt to shame.[8] The memory of a prank committed at age sixteen deals with the dominant emotion of shame, not guilt. Augustine helps you realize that early experiences of shame are internal to the self and cannot be externalized the way that guilt can. Recognizing your own unworthiness in an experience of shame enables God to uncover the darkness of your heart.

Another experience of shame that Augustine recalled was his joking about a friend's baptism shortly before the friend's death. He had just begun teaching rhetoric in his home town at about the age of nineteen or twenty. A childhood friend had contracted a fever and was in an unconscious state for a long time. When he improved temporarily, Augustine tried to joke with him about the Christian baptism that he had recently received. His friend was horrified and disturbed. Subsequently, he had a relapse and died. We can feel the shame Augustine felt as he reflected on this experience of loss.

> To myself I became a great riddle, and I questioned my soul as to why it was sad and why it afflicted me so grievously, and it could answer me nothing. . . . O deepest perversity! But such was I! My God, I do not blush to confess your mercies to me and to call upon you, I who once did not blush to profess before men all my blasphemies and to bark like a dog against you. (IV, 4 and 16)

The reference to blushing suggests the language of shame that Augustine used to expose his humiliation as one who had been consecrated to serve the Church as bishop of Hippo. By means of this process of theological reflection, he knew that as he exposed his shameful self, God was being revealed to him. Likewise, you may find that embracing your shameful self is equivalent to identifying with the shameful crucifixion of Jesus and thereby experiencing God as no longer hidden to you.

Writing his memoirs in his middle age (from age forty-three to forty-six) caused Augustine to ask the question:

What is becoming of me? The two previous life stories were representative of what he had been—a sensual materialist with a shameful life-style and a public orator with shameful insensitivity to significant others. Against this background, the master story of Augustine's conversion begins with the visit of Ponticianus (VIII, 6). It takes place during the extended period from 384 to 386 (age thirty to thirty-three) while Augustine was serving as a public orator in Milan. This high court official, who was also a Christian, tells Augustine a story of strolling through the emperor's gardens with three other men. They discover a little book about the life of the hermit Anthony of Egypt (ca. A.D. 250–356) in a house where some Christians lived. One of the men filled with "sober shame" as he began to read the book. Ponticianus describes how the man was changed within himself as he continued to read.

Augustine was deeply moved by this story, which he heard shortly before his conversion. Our translator calls his subsequent reflection "The Naked Self" (VIII, 7). As if calling to mind the Garden of Eden story of shame and defilement, the next section is entitled "In the Garden" (VIII, 8). Here Augustine begins the story of his own garden experience in Milan, in which his friend, Alypius, was by his side. The climax is reached in the description of the turning point that completely changed Augustine's life.

> I arose from Alypius's side . . . and went farther apart, so that not even his presence would be a hindrance to me. . . . And lo, I heard from a nearby house, a voice like that of a boy or a girl, I know not which, chanting and repeating over and over, "Take up and read. Take up and read. . . ." So I hurried back to the spot where Alypius was sitting, for I had put there the volume of the apostle when I got up and left him. I snatched it up, opened it, and read in silence the chapter on which my eyes first fell: "Not in rioting and drunkenness, not in chambering and impurities, not in strife and envying; but put you on the Lord Jesus Christ, and make not provision for the flesh in its concupiscences (Romans 13:13-14). (VIII, 12)

This master story, like Paul's, is another powerful example of personal transformation. An answer had been found to

Augustine's autobiographical question: What is becoming of me? Donald E. Capps answers for him: "I am becoming a person who opens himself to God."[9] The shame and reproach that Augustine felt in stealing pears and joking about a friend's baptism were removed by the determination to open himself, totally, to God.

Like the previous stories, this garden experience in Milan presents another mirror for viewing your ministry formation. Can you recall any experiences of shame that may have contributed to your conversion and/or your call to the Christian ministry? Like Paul and Augustine, your turning point, which began in a "revelatory moment," will continue to grow and develop throughout your lifetime. The ongoing process of professional development will be strengthened by examining Augustine's integration of pastoral identity. Fortunately, the *Confessions* may be studied again through Augustine's reflection on his own experience as a whole person under God. His clinical record of the interaction among "mind, soul, and will" becomes a backdrop for analyzing the formation of your pastoral identity.

THE EMERGENCE OF AN INTEGRATED PASTORAL IDENTITY

The three components of Augustine's pastoral identity will be examined with the help of a method suggested by Wayne E. Oates in relation to the doctrine of the Trinity:

> The psychological models—whether of an intrapersonal or an interpersonal nature—have historically been the analogies used by theologians to interpret the doctrine of the Trinity. . . . The changing models of selfhood, however inadequate or symbolic, were and still are used to express the unchanging nature of the Godhead as revealed in Christ.[10]

The term *intrapersonal* enables you to read the *Confessions* from the standpoint of the trinitarian forces within Augustine's personhood, which emerge full-blown in *The Trinity* (399–419).

A closer look at Augustine's conversion reveals his own trinitarian intrapersonal profile, which makes the *Confessions* a rich resource for examining your own pastoral identity. The threefold personhood of Augustine is clearly presented in the reflection on Ponticianus' story, which precedes his call to be a Christian.

> Then, during that great struggle in my inner house, which I had violently raised up against my own *soul* in our chamber, in my *heart*, troubled both in *mind* and in countenance, I turn upon Alypius and cry out to him: "What is the trouble with us? . . . Are we ashamed to follow, because they have gone on ahead of us? Is it no shame to us not even to follow them?" . . . For not only to go, but even to go in thither was naught else but the *will* to go, to *will* firmly and finally, and not to turn and toss, now here, now there, a struggle, half-maimed *will*, with one part rising upwards and another falling down. (VIII, 8, italics added)

What Augustine's "mind" understood and his "soul" and "heart" experienced was being confirmed by his "will." The intrapersonal unity of mind, soul, and will came together in his conversion, which he also understands as his Christian calling. Having found his own integrated personhood in a Milanese garden, Augustine was able to project a psychological penetration into the great mystery of the Trinity.

> Who among us understands the almighty Trinity? . . . I speak of these three: *to be, to know,* and *to will.* For *I am,* and *I know,* and *I will:* I am a knowing and a willing being, and I know that I am and that I will, and I will to be and to know. Therefore, in these three, let him who can do so perceive how inseparable a life there is, *one life,* and *one mind* and *one essence,* and finally how inseparable a distinction there is, and yet there is a distinction. (XIII, 11, italics added)

Augustine's analogy of the Trinity is based on the trinitarian nature of the self. The implication is that within each person there are three actualities: being, knowing, and willing. Therefore, a single (unitary) identity of soul, mind, and will is as close as our finite understanding can come to the mystery of one God who exists as Father, Son, and Holy Spirit.

From the depths of Augustine's psychological understanding, a picture of your pastoral identity emerges as the tripartite unity of mind, soul/heart, and will.[11] My reading of the *Confessions* has revealed the blueprint of this "trinity within man" by recording the number of times that *mind, soul/heart,* and *will* are used in each of the thirteen books. Without burdening you with the details of these word studies, the picture that emerges from Augustine's most frequent usage of these words contain three peaks: (1) Augustine's "soul/heart" is yearning for answers as he struggles in early adulthood (ages ten to twenty-eight) with the Manichean belief system (book IV); (2) His "will" is subdued in the experience of conversion in young adulthood at age thirty-two (book VIII); and (3) His "mind" finds rest in the use of his memory in the middle-age experience of actually writing the *Confessions* from ages forty-three to forty-six (book X).

From the perspective of his innermost being, the decisive battle was fought in the assertion of his will "toward God" in book VIII:

> Now to move one's bodily members at the command of the *will,* and now not to move them; now to be affected by some emotion, and now not to utter wise judgments by means of signs, and now to remain silent—such things belong to a *soul* and a *mind* that are subject to change. (VIII, 25, italics added)

The crucial struggle of the will, which led directly to Augustine's conversion, is reminscent of the subduing of Paul's will on the Damascus Road (Acts 9:3-9). It is significant that the tumultuous intrapersonal conflict of book VIII ends with a direct reference to the apostle Paul: "In a wondrous way all these things penetrated my very vitals, when I read the words of 'that least of your apostles' (I Cor. 15:9) and meditated upon your works, and trembled at them" (VII, 27).

Paul's master story is actually quoted when Augustine refers to his self-image of sensual pleasure as "kicking against the goads" (Acts 9:5; III, 8; cf. VII, 27 and VIII, 4). In the providence of God, Augustine was guided to let his eyes find the insightful words of Paul in Romans 13:13-14. This crucial passage invited him to take off his fleshly garment and to cloth himself in Christ. The change of clothing implies that he would no longer be naked, exposed before God. The words of the apostle Paul empower Augustine to put on Christ so that he can stand before God without shame.

Other references to Paul, by name or by direct quotations from his letters, suggest that Augustine's ministry model is Paul's effective style of leadership. Like Paul, his *being* (mind/soul) and *doing* (will) are highly motivated in assisting Christ with the building of his Church. Grounded in an empathetic style of leadership during the formative years of building monastic communities, he is prepared for the opposite extreme of asserting efficient pastoral leadership when necessary. For example, Peter Brown's description of Augustine's strong defense of the Church against the Donatist schism and the Pelagian heresy reads like a modern detective story.[12] The effective leadership style that was being formed in the experience of writing the *Confessions* launched a resurgence of North African Christianity that has never been surpassed. Augustine's determination to become an effective leader who is both empathetic and efficient reinforces the contribution that Paul's story has already made to your ministry formation.

THE INTENTIONAL DISCIPLINE OF REFLECTION

Because Augustine's reflection in the *Confessions* is always from a Christian perspective, it is both theological reflection and self-reflection at the same time. The two processes overlap and eventually merge in your ministry formation because all roads lead to both the self and God. The integration of self-reflection and theological reflection is implied by Augustine's epigram: "Let me know myself—Let me know Thee" (I, 1).

Augustine's integrated pastoral identity was driven by a strong will, which was informed by an inquiring mind and a sensitive heart. The extent to which he achieved a balance between performance and personhood is exemplary. His intentional balancing act is a judgment on the danger of allowing your pastoral practice to degenerate into a frenzied activism that loses touch with God. His emphasis on the Christian life as a pilgrimage toward God suggests an alternative to the harried pace of life that is characteristic of many ministers.

My own quest for being is enriched by a passion for classical music, which has been a consistent part of my ministry formation for four decades. A deep immersion in the world of opera and symphony is a reservoir that adds uniqueness to my pastoral identity. You will be a more versatile minister if you can allow your own specialty to add some seasoning to your self-reflection. Daily references to the newspaper, whether it is the sports section or the performing arts supplement, will contribute to your ministry formation.

A newspaper article in the "Arts and Leisure" supplement of the *Chicago Tribune* drew my attention to James Conlon, who was conducting the Chicago Symphony during the fiftieth anniversary season of the Ravinia Festival. This thirty-four-year-old American-born conductor, like James Levine of the Metropolitan Opera, is a personal disclaimer for the wide-spread opinion that there are no American conductors. The secret of his success is contained in an amazing reflection on his search for balance as a young conductor.

> In all his activities, Conlon sought to attain balance. "Conducting is a matter of feelings, of intellect and of physical technique, an extension of the soul, the brain and the body," he said. "What is important is to integrate them. With all the technical advances in music and technological advances in everything else, we are losing integration. When technique runs ahead of the other two areas, distortion is the result. You have got to protect the other part. You are born with gifts and limitations, but the rest is up to you."[13]

Instead of "the soul, the brain and the body," Augustine finds his balance as a pastoral leader in the soul, the mind, and the will. Your own sense of an integrated pastoral identity is the best defense you can muster against the myriad of techniques and gimmicks that can fragment the practice of your ministry.

Augustine's pastoral identity provides a perspective for attempting to balance the performance expectations of your congregation (or other ministry context) and your own personal capacity for self-reflection. This balancing act may be summarized as the inseparability of action and reflection. Action is the necessity of doing, which James Glasse has reduced to its most basic form as "paying the rent."[14] It includes the balance between mission and maintenance, between doing what is essential and what is optional, between being a pastoral generalist and developing your own ministry specialty. Reflection is the refreshment of being, which Richard Foster approaches as the *Celebration of Discipline*. It includes meditation, prayer, fasting, study, simplicity, solitude, submission, service, confession, worship, and guidance.[15]

Your reading of Augustine's *Confessions* may have the same effect on you as it did on the Italian poet Petrarch (1304–1374): "When I read your *Confessions*, I experienced two contrary affections—hope and fear, sometimes not unmingled with tears; since I account myself to be reading the narrative, not of another man's pilgrimage, but of my own."[16] You cannot take Augustine seriously without becoming more intentional about your own self-reflection.

Augustine's story also magnifies the importance of peer involvement in this process of self-reflection. His life is like a magnet, gathering around him some of the most capable men of the entire region, who eventually become fellow bishops in North Africa. Peter Brown suggests that the *Confessions* were written in order for Augustine to maintain contact with his colleagues beyond a purely African circle of bishops—such as Paulinus at Nola (in Campania, Italy) and Jerome in Bethlehem—who remained far away.[17]

The circle of friends with whom Augustine was privileged

to spend a great deal of time reads like a "Who's Who" of North African Christianity. The most prominent of these younger colleagues will be listed in relation to the friendship and/or monastic connections that brought them together. His boyhood friend and lifelong companion, Alypius, became bishop of Thagaste, Augustine's home town. His monastic companion in Cassiciacum, Aurelius, Augustine's most powerful supporter, became bishop of Carthage, the capital of Numidia. His monastic companion in Thagaste, Evodius, a retired member of the secret police, became bishop of Uzalis, a seaport near Carthage. His monastic companion in Hippo, Possidius, the only contemporary biographer of Augustine, became bishop of Calama, a town south of Hippo. Another monastic companion in Hippo, Eraclius, an efficient administrator with a taste for constructing new edifices, succeeded Augustine as bishop of Hippo.

Augustine's legacy is not only in his writings, but it is also in the lives of the young ministers that he nurtured during their formative years. His unreserved commitment as a pastoral leader is strengthened continually by critical self-reflection in dialogue with God and with significant others. The disciplines of intense contemplation with peers and intense communication with God unite in making his pastoral leadership truly effective. His intellectual inquiry about God and his personal experience with God in a close-knit community sustain his intense involvement with the church. R. L. Ottley makes the bold assertion that Augustine weds the three elements of religion—the intellectual, the experiential, and the institutional—more than any other great Christian leader.[18]

The components of your ministry formation are falling into place and will help you to become a more integrated and balanced minister. Your reading of the *Confessions* from this perspective will provide a useful review of the formation process.

Like John Mark, Augustine became keenly aware of his limitations. He reflected intensely on earlier experiences in his youth in which he failed miserably. Learning from these short-comings, he continued to shape his emerging pastoral identity.

Like Paul, he found his strength in a balanced style of leadership that combined the "being" of his mind and soul/heart with the "doing" of his will. Augustine's capacity for self-reflection provides a vocabulary that goes beyond the sketchy information that is available for an analysis of the biblical ministry models. Nevertheless both Paul and Augustine trace their pastoral authority to a decisive "transforming moment," in which they encounter God through Christ.

Augustine's integrated identity formation and commitment to Christian community add another component to the formation process—*spiritual formation.* He helps you to view your faith development as a pilgrimage of moving toward both the self and God. He reminds you that knowing yourself is possible only in relation to knowing God, that knowing yourself and God is possible only in the context of Christian community. The integration of identity formation and faith development with supportive community becomes spiritual formation.

For most ministers, the context for supportive community is the local church, especially a small membership congregation that functions as an extended family of members and adherents. Pastor Betty learned that the bonds of Christian community were even stronger in a time of crisis. Augustine learned that his spiritual and intellectual growth were enhanced by interaction with his peers in the disciplined bond of a monastic community. One of the modern versions of this kind of integrative experience is clinical pastoral education (CPE).

You have already been introduced to Wayne E. Oates, a pioneer in the CPE movement, in connection with interpreting the *Confessions* of Augustine. His Augustinian approach to spiritual formation will develop more fully this key component of the formation process. Fortunately, the awkward gap of sixteen centuries is removed by turning to the contemporary story of Professor Oates. An early, traumatic experience in his teaching career will provide another window for examining your ministry formation.

Your reflective capacities have been stimulated by the

Confessions of Augustine. Further reading of this devotional classic will be more meaningful if you ponder the questions below. They will facilitate further critical reflection on your formation process. Augustine has taught you that all reflection for the Christian minister is theological. Therefore, your self-reflection gradually will become a more integrated process.

Questions for Self-reflection

1. Why is identity formation an important aspect of pastoral leadership?

2. Why is it essential to become grounded in your Christian identity before developing a pastoral identity?

3. Is your Christian identity (like Augustine's) preceded by other self-images or vocations? If your answer is yes, describe the initial stage(s) of your identity formation.

4. Have you had other world views or philosophies of life (like Augustine) that have competed for your loyalty prior to becoming a Christian? What are the contemporary equivalents of the Manichaean or Neoplatonic world views? Would the "playboy" philosophy or humanism fit either of these categories?

5. Have you had another vocation prior to becoming a professional church leader? Do the skills you learned in this vocation (like those of Augustine) contribute to your effectiveness as a pastoral leader?

Questions for Theological Reflection

1. Can you describe the specific experience (like Augustine's) that led to your Christian calling? Was it the same as or different from your conversion experience?

2. Who are the key persons that were most influential in encouraging your Christian calling? Was the encouragement familial (like Monica's) or professional (like Ambrose's)?

3. Do you have a "spiritual friend" (like Alypius) with whom you have shared your experience of Christian calling? If your answer is no, do you feel a need for finding a "companion on the inner way" with whom you can share your ministry formation?

4. Have you had the benefit of a pastoral support group at any point during the course of your ministry formation? If your answer is no, what initiative could you take (like Augustine) in forming such a group? Is it more natural in your case to proceed informally or to work through official judicatory structures?

5. Have you (like Augustine) found an appropriate balance between the cultivation of your inner life and your more public duties as a pastoral leader? If your answer is no, which side of the scale needs more attention, being or doing?

6. Are you able to distinguish between the two aspects of being in terms of spiritual formation (soul) and intellectual development (mind)? Which receives more attention in your ministry formation? What could be done to correct the imbalance?

7. Are these inner dimensions visible in your doing (will)? Does it take all three components of the self to provide an adequate expression of pastoral authority?

8. Is there a difference between pastoral authority and pastoral leadership? Are these terms the visible side (doing) of your pastoral identity (being)?

9. Can you recall (like Augustine) any former experiences of shame that need to be integrated into your pastoral identity? Does the recognition of your "dark side" contribute to or detract from your pastoral authority?

10. Can you be a pastoral leader on the surface wihout becoming an integrated person? Can the concept of "leader" really be separated from the qualifications of "pastor"?

CHAPTER FIVE

ACCELERATING YOUR SPIRITUAL FORMATION: *WAYNE E. OATES*

Two new college students were discussing their ideal image for a husband. A starting point was deciding whether they wanted to look for a Southern boy or a Northern boy. At first, it was not easy to discern the difference, until one of the coeds explained it to the other. "A Southern boy will take you for slow walks along the path of a beautiful garden and whisper 'sweet nothings' into your ear. He is the ultimate romantic. A Northern boy will take you on fast trips and show you strange places that you have only read about. He is the bold adventurer." This clear distinction caused the insightful girl to ask her puzzled roommate, "Which do you prefer?" The answer was ingenious: "I want to find a Southern boy from as far North as possible!"

That description fits Wayne E. Oates, a South Carolinian who has spent his entire professional life very close to the Mason-Dixon line in Louisville, Kentucky. His story will introduce you to one who is known as the father of pastoral care among Baptists. Even more important is the contemporary model of ministry formation that unfolds during Wayne Oates' formative years. Reflecting on this part of his story will help you to anticipate the unavoidable detours that will surely change the direction of your ministry.

Born in Greenville, South Carolina, on June 24, 1917, Wayne Oates is the youngest of four children. He was raised by his mother, Lula, and her mother, Mary Jane, both of whom are acknowledged in the dedication of his autobiography.[1] His father abandoned the family shortly after Wayne's birth and died when Wayne was only seventeen. Growing up in the wretched poverty of a cotton mill existence required that Wayne quit school at fourteen and go to work.

Two bright spots broke the pattern of his wounded self-esteem as a teenager—serving as a page in the United States Senate for two years in Washington, D.C., and making a profession of faith in Jesus Christ. As a "babe in Christ," he was initially fed with "milk" and then with "meat" (I Corinthians 3:1-2):

> At age 16 he made a profession of faith in Jesus Christ and was baptized. It would be a few years, however, before he fully understood just what that experience meant. In the fall of 1936, with the encouragement of a Sunday School teacher, Oates entered Mars Hill College near Ashville, N.C. Under the preaching of William L. Lynch, who "conversed with me personally about the meanings, message and person of Jesus Christ," Oates claims, "this was the time of my real conversion."[2]

From Mars Hill College, he went to Wake Forest College. There he took his first course in marriage and family under the tutelage of Professor Olin T. Binkley. His classmate, Henlee Barnette, who had a similar cotton mill heritage, became a close friend. They graduated together on May 27, 1940.

Wayne's next two years were spent as pastor of two rural Baptist churches near Spring Hope, North Carolina. The part-time arrangement during the school year also made it possible for him to be an instructor in psychology and philosophy at Wake Forest College. In that rural setting, he met Pauline Rhodes, who became his wife on May 31, 1942. By then, he had left the Wake Forest area and enrolled at Duke Divinity School in Durham, North Carolina. One year of graduate study there enabled Wayne and Pauline to take classes together. He also served as a part-time associate pastor in a nearby Baptist church. The goal of going all the way to a Ph.D. before having children led them to Louisville in 1943. He not only received his doctorate, but also was invited to join the faculty of Southern Baptist Theological Seminary in 1948. His mentor during those five years was Gaines S. Dobbins, who taught church administration and the psychology of religion. More will be said later about a major struggle that complicated his early teaching career during this formative period.

The rest of his story is well known. It is divided into two periods: (1) twenty-six years until 1974 as professor of psychology of religion at Southern and (2) fourteen years until the present time as professor of psychiatry and behavioral sciences and director of the Program in Ethics and Pastoral Counseling at the University of Louisville School of Medicine, Department of Psychiatry. A 1984 "Wayne E. Oates Festival" in Louisville celebrated his return to Southern as senior professor of psychology of religion and Pastoral Care. These formal titles should not obscure the warmth of a master teacher who is best known through his prolific writing. About fifty books, plus countless articles and reviews, make the "whole" Wayne Oates almost as difficult to grasp as is the "whole" Augustine.

His life has some interesting similarities and differences with that of Augustine. Augustine was from a small town in the southern province of Africa in a highly sophisticated Roman world and always felt ill at ease in the intellectual centers of Rome and Milan. His accent called attention to his difference from the rest of the well-bred Roman citizens. For Wayne Oates, the poverty of Greenville, South Carolina, seemed like another world in comparison to the intellectual centers of Washington, D.C., and Louisville. Like Augustine, he also had the feeling of being different because of his distinctive accent. Augustine returned to his native country at the age of thirty-four and developed his life work in North Africa over the next four decades. Wayne Oates chose to leave his Carolina roots at the age of twenty-six and has developed his life work in Louisville over the subsequent five decades. Instead of writing his autobiography at the beginning of his ministerial career, as did Augustine, Professor Oates chose to tell his story at the height of his creative power. He shows no signs of tiring as a writer and is just beginning to capitalize on the resource of his own family.[3]

Wayne Oates is not easily categorized because he resists both "the clubbiness of liberals" and "the storm-trooper tactics of the fundamentalists." He is not a disciple of Sigmund Freud, Carl Rogers, Harry Stack Sullivan, or Erik Erikson. Instead of identifying with any of the popular "bandwagons" of psychotherapy, he says:

> At no point have I accepted wholesale the teachings and methods of any of them. Nor have I been an eclectic, picking and choosing this and that from each of them.
>
> To the contrary, I have used the criteria of Reformation and free-church theology for assessing the "trendiness" of each wave of crowd thinking. . . . *Protestant Pastoral Counseling* (1962) . . . put the work of pastoral counseling in relation to the life of the Spirit, the life of the church, and the hope of the Kingdom of God. It still provides my own theoretical base for pastoral counseling and psychotherapy.[4]

The freedom to be his own person is the driving force behind his extensive literary output, which is unmatched by anyone else in the field of pastoral care and counseling.

Like the spies who were surveying the land of Canaan for the first time, you may also feel like a "grasshopper" in relation to this intellectual and spiritual "giant" (Numbers 13:33). He will become a fellow struggler as you examine the crucial four years of his graduate study at Louisville and the subsequent beginning of his teaching career. His pattern of ministry formation, like that of John Mark, is more like a roller coaster than a marked trail. The way in which a graduate student handles a major disappointment will help you to become more aware of the importance of spiritual formation in the early years of your ministerial career.

REJECTION AS A CPE SUPERVISOR

It is inconceivable that one who has been so influential in the movement of clinical pastoral education (CPE) did not receive supervisory status. Yet, this part of his story will help you to face life's detours. The stage for his professional roadblock was set in relation to the struggle to be free of "pack thinking":

> Probably the most vivid encounters I have had with pack thinking . . . have been in the field of clinical pastoral education and the hand-in-glove relationship our movement has with psychiatry and psychotherapy. When I entered this field in 1944 . . . I had a remarkably wise and thought-provoking supervisor in Rev. Ralph Bonacker, who himself had been through analysis and who had a firm grasp of Reformed and Augustinian theology. Yet when I got to Chicago and Elgin State Hospital, I found men in charge of the program who were . . . in severe conflict with Anton Boisen because he resisted the bandwagon enthusiasm for popularized versions of Freud.[5]

Wayne's first quarter of CPE with Chaplain Ralph Bonacker was taken at the Norton Memorial Infirmary in Louisville. This CPE supervisor, an Episcopal priest, was theologically attuned and psychoanalytically trained. The summer basic unit of CPE was followed by an extended unit in the same hospital during the 1944–1945 academic year. Twelve hours per week for thirty-six weeks in CPE were required in addition to a full load of classes at the seminary. For this extracurricular experience, he received academic credit because of weekly reflection sessions in the evening with Dr. Dobbins.

An advanced third unit of CPE during the summer of 1945 proved to be a different kind of experience. Wayne and Pauline traveled to the Chicago area with the expectation of his working with Dr. Anton Boisen at the Elgin State Hospital. Upon arriving in Elgin, they were surprised to learn that Dr. Boisen had been defrocked as a CPE supervisor. That decision had been made by the Northeastern-Midwestern organization known as the Council for Clinical Training, the same group that had approved Chaplain Ralph Bonacker as a supervisor. Dr. Boisen remained on the staff of the hospital as a kind of chaplain emeritus. However, the newly appointed supervisor was committed to the "party line" of a Freudian psychoanalytical approach. This inexperienced supervisor found himself working wih a disappointed, hostile group of students, among whom was a Southern Baptist Seminary instructor with whom he had a first-class conflict of values as well as of authority.

Edward Thornton continues the story that rapidly moved toward an unexpected climax.

> What Wayne's supervisor at Elgin could not see, or if he saw it could not affirm, was that Wayne Oates was searching for a way to introduce the clinical approach into a seminary curriculum. Whereas the Council's way of coping with scholasticism in theological education was to withdraw from it, Wayne Oates intended to attack it, to establish a clinical beachhead, and to set seminarians free![6]

This impasse with a council-approved supervisor proved to be a preview of a far greater clash with the council itself.

> In the spring of 1946, with two quarters of full-time training behind him and two years of part-time experience as a supervisor of seminarians, Oates was ready, according to the standards then in vogue, to seek accreditation. He arranged an interview with Kuether, who was Associate Director of the Council for Clinical Training. Oates proposed to work in consultation with Bonacker in developing the clinical training program of the Seminary and requested recognition as a supervisor. Kuether rejected Oates' application, however, and offered him no alternatives for developing an indigenous program under adequate supervision.[7]

Like Dr. Boisen, his unofficial student also found himself at cross purposes with the bureaucratic system that controlled the certification of CPE supervisors in the Midwest. The restraint with which Wayne Oates describes this disappointment is evidence of his awareness of a deeper "cross purpose."

> Work with Bonacker continued with excellent results throughout 1945–46. In the spring, I began to plan for a group

> of students of my own at the Kentucky Baptist Hospital. . . .
> For this, Bonacker said, I would need the approval of the director of the Council for Clinical Training. I went to Elgin to see the director. I presented my case to him, but he said that he could not approve me as a supervisor because I had been so negative with him and the other supervisor the summer before. I did not debate the matter with him nor beg him to accept me. I simply said that this let me know firsthand where I stood with him and where he stood with me.[8]

Wayne Oates' world seemed to come crashing in on him. A familiar nursery rhyme only begins to express how he must have felt:

> Humpty Dumpty sat on a wall,
> Humpty Dumpty had a great fall,
> All the king's horses and all the king's men
> Couldn't put Humpty together again.

The pain that is involved in this kind of official rejection is rarely visible but becomes a wound that heals only over a long period of time. You will be better prepared for a major change in your career direction by reflecting on Wayne Oates' gracious acceptance of a closed door. In the depths of such disappointment, you will be drawn to a new sense of dependence on God. As Stephen has taught us, what is perceived as a total loss from one perspective becomes the beginning of a new movement from another perspective (see fig. 2). The rest of Wayne Oates' story of ministry formation will convince you that there are no meaningless, dead-end streets in the providence of God.

MAKING LEMONADE OUT OF A LEMON

The problem of Wayne Oates' rejection as a CPE supervisor became an opportunity for new curricular developments at Southern Baptist Theological Seminary. He bounced back from this unexpected change in his teaching plans by asking for permission to "do his own thing."

> I returned to Louisville, conferred with Dr. Dobbins, with the superintendent of Kentucky Baptist Hospital, H. L. Dobbs, and with the president of the seminary, Dr. Ellis A. Fuller. All three agreed that the thing to do was to start our own local program of clinical pastoral education without any need for alliance with the Council for Clinical Training. Our decision was to integrate the work into the curriculum of the Southern Baptist Theological Seminary and to make the leadership of the program completely answerable academically to the faculty of the seminary and clinically to the medical staff and administration of the hospitals where we worked.
>
> . . . From then on, as far as my function with the council was concerned, the whole matter was a closed book.[9]

The controversy with the council had been turned into a coalition of curricular reform. An alternative to "factory education" was emerging and would soon expand to include other hospitals and seminaries throughout the Southern Baptist Convention.

Wayne Oates' final year of doctoral study was given focus by the persistent conviction that both Freud and the Christian faith had been badly served by the Council of Clinical Training. The importance of keeping clinical pastoral education in creative tension with the seminary curriculum needed to be defended. Therefore, Wayne Oates' doctoral dissertation became an effort to create dialogue between the work of Sigmund Freud and the Christian faith.[10]

A faculty appointment in 1948, along with J. Estill Jones and other "young Turks," strengthened the beachhead that Wayne Oates had established at Southern Baptist Theological Seminary. His influence began to be felt on a broader ecumenical front as a member of the CPE Committee of Twelve in the early 1950s. The task of this committee is to set standards for a federation of CPE agencies and programs. As a representative of the Association of Seminary Professors in the Practical Fields, he learned firsthand that the two dominant groups were the Council for Clinical Training and the Institute of Pastoral Care. His presence added at least moral support for the "third force" of the Lutheran Advisory

Council. The pioneer work of the Committee of Twelve would come to fruition fifteen years later.

In the meantime, Southern Baptist Theological Seminary became the hub of an indigenous seminary program that developed its own ties with other nearby clinical training centers. Similar clinical training programs were established in Winston Salem, North Carolina, and in New Orleans. The catalyst for bringing these centers together was the awareness in 1956 that Southern Baptist professors and chaplains who were active in clinical pastoral education did not have a voice in the unification movement. In 1957, these persons united to form the Southern Baptist Association for Clinical Pastoral Educators. The denominational "third force" in clinical pastoral education was significantly strengthened by the unification of Southern Baptist programs. The new organization succeeded in strengthening an emerging professional identity among widely scattered, clinically trained, theological educators in the South. Widely interpreted as an obstacle to unification at the time, the earlier rebuff by the Council for Clinical Training left Wayne little choice but to go his own separate way.

Beginning in 1956, four agencies formed a new Advisory Council, which replaced the old Committee of Twelve. Wayne continued to play a vital role as a representative from the new Southern Baptist Association for Clinical Pastoral Educators. In 1967, the new organization was fully assimilated as an equal partner in the new *Association for Clinical Pastoral Education, Inc.* (ACPE). The new unified movement even accepted the name of the (Southern Baptist) Association for Clinical Pastoral Educators as the umbrella designation, except for the change of Educat*ors* to Educa*tion*. In addition to the Southern Baptist group, the 1967 merger also brought together the professional identities of the original groups: the Council for Clinical Training, the Institute of Pastoral Care, and the Lutheran Advisory Council. The historic beginning of ACPE in 1967 was graced by the healing words of Wayne E. Oates:

> The Clinical Pastoral Education movement has yearned for the merger that is at hand. The pull of the current of history is against us unless we decide for ourselves to bring this merger into port. The trivialities that divide us, the old wounds that hurt in bad weather—all of which beset us—these and every other weight that holds us back should be laid aside for a higher communion in a common cause. . . . Many of our breakdowns in the past have arisen from the attempt to superimpose one culture on another rather than to develop indigenous adaptations of a common commitment to the care of the broken and sick by means of a common method.[11]

The story of a graduate theological student who received a lemon and decided to make lemonade was complete in the 1967 merger, except for a *post script*. The geographical move of the ACPE headquarters from New York City to Atlanta in 1984 would not have been possible without the Southern Baptist contribution to the "third force" in the movement.

LEARNING FROM LIFE'S DETOURS

The hindsight of Christian faith inspired the saying: "When God closes a door, he opens a window." For Wayne Oates, a painful experience of exclusion was not the end but the beginning of a new phase of ministry. In writing about *Life's Detours,* he gives you a perspective for recovering from any experience that seems like a dead-end street.

> The direction we are going is largely affected by the way we interpret the things that happen to us. Our perception of things has a powerful effect upon what those things in fact turn out to be. . . .
>
> The great griefs of life are often *not* the loss of someone by death . . . some divorced persons I know have seen their temptations for what they were—to let their broken marriage become a stuttering, sputtering broken record that could play only one note . . .
>
> On the other hand, I have seen both men and women stand back from the pieces of their life's work, gain a whole new perspective, and reorganize their lives around a new purpose for which God had called them.[12]

Without denying the reality of grief that accompanies any significant loss, you need to mobilize the resource of your faith for a second opinion about any problem. Such a crisis experience definitely calls for more than an impulsive knee-jerk reaction; it suggests the need for a period of contemplation in which a conclusion is reached after much prayer and thought. This kind of reflection is "grist for the mill" of spiritual formation. Wayne Oates learned this faith dimension well from Anton Boisen:

> Boisen was one of my teachers. . . . He became one of the first mental hospital chaplains. He was convinced that theology should be studied, not after the experiences which gave it birth had been written in the books and the books were gathering dust on the library shelf. Theology, the study of the ways of God with men as they seek their way in life's pilgrimage in a wilderness of the lost, should be studied when these experiences are actually happening to people. Persons themselves are the textbooks of the theological inquiry. They are "the living human documents."[13]

The presence of the defrocked supervisor who remained as chaplain emeritus at the Elgin State Hospital during the summer of 1945 kept Wayne Oates in the reorganized CPE program. No textbook could have prepared him as well as did this "living human document" for his own unexpected and disappointing experience of losing face by not receiving supervisory status. In both cases, God used closed doors to open windows, which ultimately strengthened the unified CPE movement. Edward Thornton speaks without reservation of the strategic role of his mentor in this unification process: "Undoubtedly the central figure in the development of clinical pastoral education in the South was Wayne E. Oates of the Southern Baptist Theological Seminary in Louisville."[14]

A crucial turning point in the life of Wayne Oates may help you to negotiate your own detours in life. His reflective orientation will encourage you to experiment with the art of spiritual formation. You cannot ignore that "the Lord Jesus Christ's own experiences with detours . . . show that dying to our old way of life and being raised to walk in the newness of life is *the* great detour of human existence."[15] That insight is the heart of spiritual formation. You were introduced to this reflective aspect of your ministry in the previous chapter. Its importance will be reinforced by the model of Wayne Oates, who, perhaps unconsciously, followed the Augustinian approach to spiritual formation.

MODELING AN AUGUSTINIAN PATTERN OF SPIRITUAL FORMATION

You know that a picture is worth a thousand words. Wayne Oates' life may be viewed as a working model of the Augustinian approach to ministry formation. If the names and places are not familiar to you, you will want to supply the equivalent names and places from your own experience in order to complete the various parts of the picture. Your composite picture should contain at least one spiritual friend, one professional mentor, yourself as a potential spiritual companion, and the other persons who have contributed to your pilgrimage in a special way. Oates' "picture" will suggest what the key components of your particular pilgrimage might look like. Use it as a rough sketch for drawing your own working model of ministry formation.

Finding a Spiritual Friend

The first step beyond your own personal discipline of prayer, meditation, and reflection is the sharing of your dreams and struggles with another person. Usually, this person is given to you on the basis of similar interests and aspirations. Your only tasks are to recognize and to cultivate this gift, perhaps for an entire lifetime.

The life-long devotion between Augustine and his loyal friend, Alypius, has been identified as a theme that can be traced throughout the *Confessions* (VI: 11-17, 21-22, 26; VIII: 13, 28-30; IX: 7, 17-37). Growing up together in Thagaste, Alypius was younger than Augustine and outlived his faithful friend. They, together, experienced the traumatic end of the Roman Empire.

Wayne Oates found a similar life-long friend in Henlee Barnette. Rooted in the same Carolina cotton mill culture of poverty, they became acquainted in 1936 as fellow mill workers at the Cannon Towel Company in Kannapolis, North Carolina. They became classmates at Wake Forest College in 1938, where they, together, took Greek, Latin, Shakespeare, psychology, and philosophy. Their pilgrimage continued in tandem as they both became students and then professors at Southern Baptist Theological Seminary (one in the psychology of religion and pastoral care and the other in Christian ethics) for over twenty years. Their friendship continues to this day as fellow professors in the University of Louisville School of Medicine and as senior professors at Southern.

Like the dark clouds of war that disrupted the peaceful environment of Augustine and Alypius during the collapse of the Roman Empire, Wayne Oates and Henlee Barnette were drawn closer together in common opposition to the Vietnam war.

> In the time span of 1968 through 1969, I experienced a serious disenfranchisement of my life in relation to the Vietnam War. . . . By September of 1968, my own son was a machine gunner in the Riverine Assault Group of Naval Inshore Operations. . . . He went through the surrealistic Apocalypse II and returned with two Purple Hearts but in excellent health, thanks to outstanding medical care.
>
> . . . My colleague, Henlee Barnette had a son . . . who refused to be drafted and fled to Sweden. Barnette and I swam through a sea of helpless rage over this situation.[16]

The loyalty and devotion expressed through these ancient and contemporary friendships represent fixed points of mutual support on long-term spiritual journeys. If you have not recognized the gift of a spiritual friend, that person should be at the center of your group picture.

Finding a Professional Mentor

The search for a senior colleague who can assist you with the unique challenges of your ministry formation is the next step on your spiritual pilgrimage. Perhaps this person has already been given to you during the course of your previous training. If not, you will be doing someone a favor by providing the occasion for that person to experience the ultimate challenge of adult development—becoming a mentor. Christian ministry adds a spiritual dimension to this mentor relationship; you can profit from the experience and wisdom of a professional mentor who has "learned the ropes." You will also need this kind of guidance when you stumble and fall during the course of your early ministry practice.

You recall that Augustine's initial ministry model was Ambrose, the revered bishop of Milan. According to Peter Brown, "The influence of Ambrose on Augustine is far out of proportion of any direct contact which the two men may have had."[17] Ambrose remained Augustine's hero throughout his entire life. At a time in his old age when Augustine felt the need for reassurance after the misbehavior of one of his protégés, he urged a Milanese deacon, Paulinus, to write a life of Ambrose. The former bishop of Milan had been dead for twenty-five years but was still having an impact on the life of his follower.

Wayne Oates had the added benefit of two mentors—Olin T. Binkley (professor of religion at Wake Forest College and subsequently professor of Christian ethics at Southern) and Gaines S. Dobbins (the father of the pastoral care movement at Southern). After transferring from Mars Hill College in order to finish his last two years at Wake Forest, Wayne was given a mentor by God, whose influence and encouragement sent him on the path toward enlarging the horizons of pastoral care. This key person also influenced Wayne's call to the Christian ministry.

> Olin Binkley was my first counselor in *any* professional sense of the word.
>
> . . . From my identification with him as a teacher I resolved to express my ministry through the classroom and the clinic as well as through the pulpit. Olin Binkley was my mentor and teacher, my confidant and friend.[18]

Wayne's second mentor, Gaines Dobbins, taught him how to develop a strategy of needs assessment in the organizational development of pastoral care.

> In the development of a ministry of pastoral care, Gaines Dobbins used a more prophetic and less bureaucratic approach to needs assessment. In the tradition of Jeremiah, he conducted "a listening-in campaign" among former students and present students in the years between 1937 and 1943. They reported the need for more equipment during their seminary years in the direct pastoral ministry to persons in the context of their daily pastoral practice.[19]

The emerging ability of Dr. Dobbins' assistant resulted in a further advancement in 1947 to the supervision of Ph.D. candidates, which taught Wayne the hazards and hopes of graduate supervision. This apprenticeship was recognized and rewarded by his appointment to the faculty in 1948. That honor was due largely to two professional mentors, who had modeled the highest ideals of a teaching ministry toward which Wayne aspired.[20]

Becoming a Spiritual Companion

I hope you have experienced the support of a spiritual friend and have learned from the guidance of a professional mentor. These experiences will qualify you eventually to become a spiritual companion. A growing body of literature is emerging, which will be helpful to those persons who want to engage in spiritual guidance.[21] The developmental term *mentor* is expanded by the vision of a spiritual companion who attempts to view all of ministry from the perspective of balancing self-reflection with theological reflection. Have you considered what it might mean to shift the emphasis of your ministry from receiving to giving, from being mentored to becoming a mentor? Your nurturing of a younger colleague will be more rewarding to you personally if you are willing to share your own spiritual journey. Perhaps the greatest contribution you can make in the Christian ministry is the energy that is expended in the spiritual formation of "sons [and daughters] of encouagement" (Acts 4:36).

Augustine's track record in this regard is impressive. Like Augustine, Wayne Oates has been the spiritual companion for a growing team of pastoral care professionals whose influence has spread throughout the United States, especially in the Southeast. Richard Young and Andrew Lester went to North Carolina Baptist Hospital in Winston Salem. Myron Madden went to Southern Baptist Hospital in New Orleans. Samuel Southard, Joseph Knowles, and Edward Thornton developed and sustained the Institute of Religion in Houston. Subsequently, Samuel Southard went to Fuller Theological Seminary. Richard Hester went to Philips University Graduate School of Theology in Oklahoma before he became the first full-time pastoral care professor at Southeastern Baptist Theological Seminary in Wake Forest, North Carolina. Edward Thornton and Albert Meiberg developed the pastoral care program at Crozer Theological Seminary in Chester, Pennsylvania. They were vital persons in the merger of Colgate Rochester Divinity School with Bexley Hall in Rochester, New York. Subsequently, Edward Thornton returned to Southern and Albert Meiberg to Southeastern. Robert Crapps became a professor of pastoral care at Furman University in Greenville, South Carolina. Liston Mills established a pastoral care presence as a professor at Vanderbilt University in Nashville, Tennessee. Roy Woodruff became a professor of pastoral care at Midwestern Baptist Theological Seminary in Kansas City, Missouri. Grayson Tucker and William Van Arnold made their contribution at Louisville Presbyterian Seminary and Union Theological Seminary in Richmond, Virginia. Edward Thornton, Andrew Lester, and Wade Rowatt became the second generation of teaching faculty at Southern, along with Walter Jackson, who administers theological field education. Richard L. Hester confirms the spiritual sensitivity of Wayne Oates' relationship with his many followers: "I learned from Oates . . . that issues of faith, in Tillich's sense of ultimate concern, are always the central ones." As if trying to keep the contemplative ideal of spiritual discipline before his younger colleagues, Wayne Oates echoed Augustine's *Confessions* by sending a message to his closest companions who are far and near.

> In the face of this concern for the practice of the presence of the Spirit, I wrote my small book *Nurturing Silence in a Noisy Heart* (1979). It reflects much of my struggle to be free of loneliness. Yet the central issue is that we are not only made for community; at base, as Augustine said, we are made by God for fellowship with God, and our hearts are restless until we find that fellowship with God.[22]

The small book mentioned above is an excellent point of departure if you desire to move from being guided spiritually to becoming a spiritual companion yourself. By shifting the emphasis of your ministry from receiving to giving, you will eventually develop your own list of future ministers who will be strengthened by your spiritual guidance.

Recognizing Other Special Persons

The group picture of your journey thus far may include only professional persons with whom you share a common theological orientation. It is not possible to contain the work of God within this limited circle. Other persons, such as family and friends, have contributed in significant ways to your minsitry formation and, therefore, need to be recognized. You will know who these persons are in your own experience. Some clues may be found in other experiences, which Augustine and Wayne Oates share.

A natural starting point is your immediate family. Augustine wrote the *Confessions*, among other reasons, as a tribute to his mother, Monica, and to his paternal grandmother (V: 13-15). Likewise, Wayne Oates dedicated his autobiography to the memory of his mother, Lula, and to his paternal grandmother. The recognition of the formative role of mothers and grandmothers is closely tied to an acceptance of their places of geographical origin. Both mothers had a conspicuous southern drawl, from which early patterns of speech were passed on to their children. Oates acknowledges this influence when he says: "To this day, I retain a Southern drawl, the graphic figures of speech, the proverbial sayings, and the directness of speech in the language of my daily work."[23] The strong encouragement of his mother enabled the young Wayne, like the youthful Augustine, to adjust to the expectations of far away intellectual centers. The overwhelming adjustment of a South Carolina lad in Washington, D.C., as a page in the United States Senate, would not have been possible without the moral support of a devoted mother. This personal indebtedness is confirmed in his autobiography: "As my mother put it: 'You have got sense enough to get out of anything you get into if you don't want to stay in it.' For a long time this comment has been the story of my life in a proverb."[24] The writing of his autobiography was itself an experience of therapy in which Oates, like Augustine, acknowledged the providence of God, which is supremely evident in the watchcare that was exercised through the loving devotion of his mother and his paternal grandmother.

Other persons may come to mind from your childhood and youth. The steps leading to Augustine's conversion include the loss of a close personal friend (IV: 7-11). As a student at Wake Forest College in his early twenties, Wayne Oates also described the loss of his roommate, Clyde Randolph, with equal poignancy.

> While reading Tennyson's *In Memoriam* I first detected the process of grief as the poet moved from the stage of shock, to disbelief, to fantasy, to despair, to stabbing memories, to a life of faith in the face of not knowing. Tennyson grieved for Arthur Hallam, his close friend. Pneumonia had that spring killed my roommate, Clyde Randolph, and I grieved for him.[25]

These experiences of loss may remind you of someone very special, whose trust and understanding contributed in a meaningful way to your spiritual formation.

The group picture of your spiritual pilgrimage should be complete at this point. The names and places connected with your journey are unique and have contributed in significant ways to your formation. Yet the impact of your spiritual friend, your professional mentor, and other special persons adds considerable momentum to the way in which your ministry formation is developing. Your indebtedness needs to be expressed in a life of service to others, especially younger colleagues who can eventually learn from you the art of spiritual companionship.

Being a mentor from the perspective of spiritual guidance calls for another look at your own spiritual journey. Other writings of Wayne Oates will enable your literary spiritual companion to suggest some of the tools that may be used on your pilgrimage.

BEGINNING YOUR OWN SPIRITUAL JOURNEY

The encouragement of Augustine and the modeling of Wayne Oates provide the impetus for you to begin your own spiritual journey. The steps that follow are suggestive of an ongoing process that will be enhanced by the check and balance of your own spiritual companion.

Confess Your Limitations

Both Augustine and Wayne Oates confront you with the inescapable fact that "confession is good for the soul." Both are remembered by their vast majority of readers for a single work that popularized this universal human need—Augustine's *Confessions* and Oates' *Confessions of a Workaholic.*[26] Augustine defines *confession* as "accusation of ourself, praise of God." This one word, which sums up his attitude to the human condition, became the new key of the Middle Ages for unlocking the riddle of evil. Wayne Oates expanded upon his own personal confession in order to define a major human condition of contemporary professional life, the tension between workaholism and grace. John

McClanahan's book review of Wayne Oates' autobiography speaks to every young minister.

> In an earlier book, Oates coined a new word—"workaholic"—which has now become a part of the American vernacular. In this book, Oates again writes perceptibly about his struggle to be free from overcommitment. Every parish minister could well read his comments about the forces which push us toward the fictitious, and even idolatrous, goal of trying to be omnipresent.[27]

The literary affinity between these two prodigious authors is most obvious in relation to the one word—*confession.* Although an interpersonal approach to spiritual companionship begins with *friendship* and *comfort,* the deeper level of *confession* and *instruction* should follow.[28] You may find it easier to deal with the confession of your limitations before focusing on the self-accusation of wrongdoings in the Augustinian sense. In either case, your confession will be balanced with praise to God.

Decide on Your Goal

Your capacity for serious reflection opens the door to an ongoing spiritual journey. A play on words will help you to discern the goal of your pilgrimage. Augustine's *Confessions* are "The Struggle to Find Rest." Wayne E. Oates' *The Struggle to Be Free* is an updating of his "Confessions" (*Confessions of a Workaholic*). The key difference in these two autobiographies is between finding rest and being free, two complementary ways of expressing the goal of centering, or focusing, life in Christ. The steps that lead to this goal will provide you with a basic framework for your own spiritual formation.

The choice to move away from your goal is "wandering." The double meaning in Augustine's use of *peregrinatio* signifies initially the soul's movement away "from God." Wayne Oates uses this term in the same way: "[Everyone's] 'primitively planned' selfhood is . . . a *wandering,* disrupted, isolated, and sin-laden identity. . . . The self is no longer a *wandering,* searching identity [when it] has found its true dwelling place in Christ."[29] At a subconscious level, Augustine's masterpiece has been assimilated to the extent that it is a natural part of Wayne Oates' self-expression.

The choice to move toward your goal is "pilgrimage." This alternate way in which Augustine uses *peregrinatio* describes the soul's movement back "toward God." Likewise, Oates follows the Augustinian usage of this term:

> The *pilgrimage* of encounter with Christ on the part of the Christian community is in itself an historical treasure of psychological wisdom. . . . [Psychoanalytic] truths can be entered by the Christian theologian into his understanding of the lonely *pilgrimage* of people from diffuse identity to defined selfhood.[30]

The subtle play on the Latin word *peregrinatio* can represent your wandering from God or your pilgrimage toward God.

Finally, arriving at your goal of spiritual centering is "rest." Augustine uses this term for the soul's return from alienation to the wholeness that is experienced "in God." From his perspective, the goal of the Christian life is to find rest for the pilgrim *(peregrinus),* who is a temporary resident on this earth. Therefore, your true Christian identity is as a citizen of heaven in the city of God. Normal human society is made up of those who are aware of being different as "resident strangers" *(civitas peregrina).* Augustine experienced this alien situation in both Rome and Milan. Wayne Oates was also a "resident stranger" in Washington, D.C., and Louisville, but he came to the realization that freedom in Christ was his true "focus," which literally means "hearth" or "home." "In Jesus Christ and the Holy Spirit God has come to the self and made his home in the self. . . . The old self was a *stranger,* but the new self [is] now a fellow citizen in the household of God."[31] However you choose to define the goal, you will need to be brutally honest about whether you are moving toward it or away from it. Your own spiritual journey will be enriched as you experiment with the particular disciplines that help you to structure your movement toward the goal of finding rest or being free.

Follow a Prescribed Pattern

Now the goal of focusing your life in Christ has been established. Next, you need to follow a prescribed pattern of particular disciplines. The Augustinian model includes the fourfold process of movement toward the self, rest in the self, movement toward God, and rest in God. This approach to spiritual formation is latent in Wayne Oate's *Christ and Selfhood*. His reflections suggest a strategy for your own spiritual formation.

The first stage of movement "toward the self" begins with the "good confession" in which you can stand as a self "in the presence of many witnesses," as I Timothy 6:12 says. The second stage of focus (or rest) "in the self" follows quite naturally as a result of the previous movement. It is at this point that the ridiculously difficult simplicity of the secret of selfhood will be revealed: "For whoever wants to save his life will lose it, but whoever loses his life for me will save it" (Luke 9:24). The third stage of movement "toward God" is acknowledged explicitly.

> An irreconcilable tension exists, because man, as Augustine says, is made "toward God". . . . Only the truth that edifies is the truth. The renunciation of the immaturities of craftiness and deceitfulness issues in the kind of growth that is, as Augustine says, "toward God" in Christ."[32]

The fourth stage of focus (or rest) "in God" is the goal of the Christian's pilgrimage. Wayne Oates describes in his autobiography what it means to celebrate life "in God."

> For me, the quality of a certain kind of loneliness necessitates the fellowship with God which transforms loneliness into solitude. Augustine spoke of God as "Thou, Almighty, who art with me, yea, before I am with thee" (*Confessions*, Book X, Sec. 6). I have chosen to be concerned for this *beforeness* in my vocation as a practical mystic in the maelstrom of events that flow over my awareness. The act of concern of being alone with God turns loneliness into solitude, contemplation, and fellowship with God.[33]

His autobiography confirms the earlier observation: "In Jesus Christ and the Holy Spirit God has come to the self and made his home in the self."

The importance that both Augustine and Wayne Oates place on spiritual formation should be an encouragement to you. An intentional approach to this discipline will guarantee the continuation of ministry formation throughout your lifetime.

Keep A Positive Attitude

You will need to be reminded at many points on your journey that the autobiographies of Augustine and Wayne Oates are characterized by a positive attitude toward life, regardless of outward circumstances that could suggest the acceptance of defeat. Both have an eternally optimistic outlook on human nature. You will want to return for encouragement to the way John McClanahan characterizes Oates' tendency to find the best in a bad situation and to see the hidden potential in every person.

> Wayne Oates has spent a professional lifetime learning to read the lives of other people as living human documents—like authentic primary sources—for discovering the truth and beauty, the pain and glory, which is inherent in every human being. Each person's life is a book from which [you] may discover something good, if [you] will but learn to listen and heed. How many times have students in his classes heard Professor Oates declare, "Even the clock that doesn't run is right twice a day!"[34]

One who has recovered from an experience of failure is more likely to see the potential for growth and development in another person. Whether it is Augustine's frustrating year of teaching in Rome or Wayne Oates' disappointing encounter with the Council for Clinical Training, both men picked up the pieces and kept on going. You are likely to have similar experiences of severe testing, in which you may be tempted "to throw in the towel." A universal axiom of spiritual formation insists that there is no such thing as a bad experience; you can learn from every frustration, disappointment, and failure. William Malcomson is correct in writing that *Success Is a Failure Experience.*[35] You will find that your spiritual formation takes on new meaning as your own resources collapse and your dependence on God catches fire. Instead of failure, you will find the freedom to become your own person.

Your new sense of realism may even prompt a smile or a laugh. Wayne Oates has a knack for expressing this light touch: "I am a fairly weather-beaten veteran at being tempted to 'slush' my own ideals . . . laughter is at times a kind of forgiveness."[36] Accepting reality and keeping a positive attitude are two poles that must be held in creative tension throughout the course of your spiritual journey. Lest you are prone to limit reality to the inner life, Wayne Oates ends his autobiography with a call to responsible action in whatever context God has called you to serve:

> The years of later maturity for me, then, I pray, will be years of magic laughter at the multitude of things, behaviors of other people, and tides of human politics that are beyond our control, and of canny alertness to those situations which, with a little bit of luck and a massive demonstration of Providence, we can actually do something about.[37]

His story will help you to accelerate your spiritual formation. The goal is not self-serving. His kind of "canny alertness" will enable many ministers to "become mentors even as [you] have been given mentors by God."

The goal of ministry formation is, therefore, effective leadership. All of the previous stories have helped to clarify the issues of your ministry formation. Now you are in touch with your limitations. They are no longer immobilizing but an integral part of your uniqueness. A deeper awareness of your style of leadership provides the confidence to refine your pastoral identity by building on your unique strength. The integrative discipline of spiritual formation will help you to reconcile the person you are with the minister you want to become. The more you are involved in service to others, the more you will need to renew a right spirit within yourself. For descriptive purposes, this introspective task has been approached both as self-reflection and as theological reflection.

In reality, these inner processes are inseparable in Christian ministry. They find outward expression in pastoral authority and become visible in your style of leadership. You will not be satisfied if it is just empathetic. You do not want it to be just efficient. With God's help, you are on the way to becoming an effective leader.

The importance of your role within the larger kingdom enterprise cannot be overemphasized. Finding a balance in ministry between being and doing is the formula for finding *the fulfillment factor*. You will not be successful in ministry unless you find yourself challenged and feel fulfilled. Some concluding observations will point you on the way to an experience of satisfaction in the particular place you have been called to serve.

Questions for Self-reflection

1. Why is spiritual formation an important aspect of pastoral leadership? What is the relationship between spiritual formation and "burnout"?

2. Can you identify the most crushing blow in your early stage of ministry formation? Did it tend to reaffirm your assurance that "underneath are the everlasting arms" (Deuteronomy 33:27 KJV), or did you have the feeling of abandonment by God?

3. How has God's plan for your life changed because of this traumatic experience? Can you look back and discern whether "God intended it for good to accomplish what is now being done" (Genesis 50:20)?

4. Have you found a spiritual friend with whom you can share the current struggles and challenges of your ministry formation? Do you have a regular time of meeting, or is the pattern of getting together more spontaneous?

5. Whom do you most admire as a professional role model of Christian ministry? Have you considered the need that this person may have to become a mentor? Would it be easier to take the initiative in raising the question of your need for a professional mentor if you knew that it could be mutually helpful?

Questions for Theological Reflection

1. Have you considered the contribution that you may be able to make by becoming a spiritual companion with a fellow traveler on the road of ministry formation? How do your experiences with a spiritual friend and a professional mentor prepare you for this integrative task?

2. Are there other special persons who have contributed in significant ways to your ministry formation? Are they within and/or beyond your immediate family?

3. What are the dissatisfactions that need to be confessed at this stage of your spiritual journey? What are the satisfactions that give you the greatest sense of fulfillment in ministry?

4. Have you decided on a goal for engaging in spiritual disciplines? Are you primarily a verbal person, or would you consider the rigorous discipline of writing a spiritual journal?

5. Do you have a prescribed pattern of working on this task? Can you separate the academic study of the Bible from the devotional use of the Bible? Would you be aided in this task by comparing your struggle with that of a spiritual friend?

6. Is it possible to keep a positive attitude in terms of spiritual formation when there are so many other demands on your limited time and energy? Are you in control of your schedule, or is it largely determined by external circumstances?

7. How can you turn the failure of your desire to develop spiritual disciplines into a success experience? Do you need to draw most heavily on the resource of your mind, your soul, or your will?

8. Are you expecting to be a "thirty-day wonder" of spiritual maturity, or are you prepared for an ongoing reflective process "over the long haul"?

9. What is the difference between "priming the pump" and drawing deeply from the well? How do these images relate to your spiritual formation?

10. What is the relationship of spiritual formation to your priestly and prophetic roles? What does it mean to work at "inviting the mystic, supporting the prophet"?

CONCLUSION

JOHN A. MACKAY DESCRIBES TWO APPROACHES TO CHRISTIAN MINistry by picturing observers sitting on the high front balcony of a Spanish house and travelers who go by on the road below.[1] You may have been more like a "balconeer" at the beginning of this journey, having watched other ministers from a safe distance. From this perspective, problems are mainly theoretical, and solutions are tentative. By now, you should feel more like a traveler, one whose problems have been identified and whose solutions are emerging from the unexpected crises of life. This book has been written for travelers, and it has dealt with the questions that must be asked on the journey of ministry formation.

As one traveler talking to another along the way, I must say that our journey is almost over. Yet, there are four guidelines, or road signs, that will help you to get the most from your continuing pilgrimage. They have to do with the rate of speed, the element of surprise, the normality of transitions, and the importance of persistence.

TAKE YOUR TIME

Most ministers at the entry level are impatient and want a high speed journey that will get them quickly to the destination of appearing to be a polished professional. There are no magical "fast tracks" on this journey. It takes time to become an effective leader. You must get beyond a theoretical understanding of the needed balance between empathy and efficiency. The view from the balcony assumes that you are already the perfect model of a balanced and effective leader, who is sensitive to the personhood and performance demands of ministry. Instead, the road you have traveled thus far has provided a variety of successes and failures. You may have been empathetic when you needed to be efficient or vice versa.

The exercises of reflecting on your ups and downs have guided you into the experience of ministry formation. You have traveled far enough by now in order to pause and examine a sign along the road, which will tell you where you are. It is in the form of an empty cross, because your journey has been in tandem with the resurrected Christ. This directional sign is pointing downward to the spot where you are at the moment. It is like a historical marker and summarizes the stages of your journey thus far. In order to help you interpret the "markings,"[2] some guidelines are placed on either side of the sign for your information. They will help you to recall the issues of ministry formation that are inseparable from the processes for dealing with them. In either case, the directional arrows pointing downward suggest your staying put until you have examined this marker very carefully. Your grounding starts in the upper triangle with *awareness;* it proceeds through the middle rectangle of *competence;* and it leads to the lower, inverted triangle of *satisfaction* (see fig. 13).

You will recognize the middle section of the marker as the goal of a balanced and effective style of leadership (see fig. 1). The rectangular shape itself signifies at least a measure of competence in arriving at a balance between your natural gift and a learned skill. That inner struggle of the self has been arrived at by the reality orientation of testing your limitations. This awareness has emerged from an assessment of your identity formation, faith development, and pastoral authority. Getting inside your being leads naturally to how you express yourself in doing. Learning to express your underdeveloped side is represented by the dotted line of the

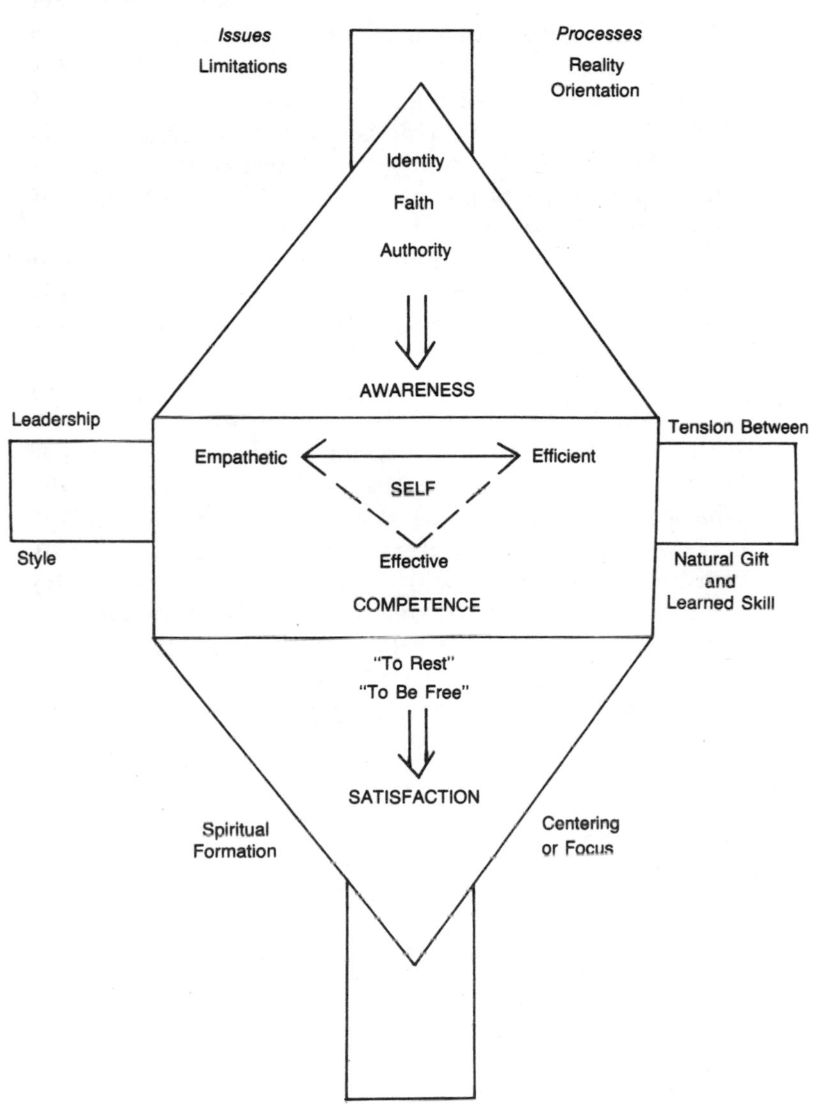

A Model of Ministry Formation (fig. 13)

inner triangle. One side is your natural gift; the other is your learned skill. Only you can make a solid line out of the one that is perceived as your unique strength. The recognition and refinement of the other side holds the key to your becoming an effective leader.

The action orientation of ministry involvement leads to the necessity of reflection. Your spiritual formation is enhanced and accelerated by the process of centering, or focusing, your life in Christ. The ease with which you are relaxing, instead of overcompensating, is giving you a growing sense of satisfaction. You are at the point of celebrating a rest stop on your journey, in which you can be free of the need for over achievement.

These checkpoints on your journey—awareness, competence, and satisfaction—can be internalized as the current stage of your ministry formation. They will be refined through further experience. They will become the essence of what you will have to share as a spiritual companion. Your experience as a traveler will enable you to describe in specific terms your relationship with God as Father, Son, and Holy Spirit. You will be able to explain both the times of *wandering* "from God" and the restorations of forgiveness and grace that enable you to resume your *pilgrimage* "toward God."

The first sign has fine print that forces you to take a rest stop and to focus on every word. This crucial marker interprets the nature of your journey. It forces you to develop your patience so that you will be content to take your time. The Oriental version of its message is "Don't push the river." The other markers are like caution signs along the way, which will help you to keep a steady but unhurried pace.

EXPECT MANY SURPRISES

You may find yourself needing the exhortation "Expect a Miracle," which greets me in the form of a desk placque on each new day. The task of ministry formation is not predictable. It must remain open to many surprises. Beginning with the two dimensions of time and space, the ultimate goal of knowing God is a three dimensional world that also includes eternity. The element of surprise allows eternity to break into time and space in such a way that your story is enriched by the mystery of God's story. That is *The Meaning of Revelation,* according to H. Richard Niebuhr. It is "not only progressive but it requires of those to whom it has come that they begin the never-ending pilgrim's progress of the reasoning Christian heart."[3] Whether on the balcony or on the road, unexpected vistas lie ahead on your journey of ministry formation.

> [You] climb the mountain of revelation that [you] may gain a view of the shadowed valley in which [you] dwell and from the valley [you] look up again to the mountain. Each arduous journey brings new understanding, but also new wonder and surprise. This mountain is not one [you] climbed once upon a time; it is a well-known peak [you] never wholly know, which must be climbed again in every generation, on every new day.[4]

The end of your ongoing journey is unknown, but three of the surprises are projected, by Timothy George, from the Augustinian perspective of pilgrimage.

> Pilgrimage . . . suggests the following ideals:
>
> 1. Sanctified ambiguity. Abraham "went out not knowing whither he went."
> 2. Community of co-strugglers. No one can be a pilgrim alone.
> 3. Witness in via. We are a community of learning, but also a community of grace and love, sharing the light we have received with everyone else we meet on the road, even as we continue to look for the City which hath foundations.[5]

Pilgrims on the road of ministry formation will remain open to ambiguity. They will explore the interpersonal dimension of spirituality. They will not be afraid of giving expression to spontaneity. The trail will be marked not only with surprises, but will also consist of unexpected turns along the way.

MONITOR YOUR TRANSITIONS

You will want to give special attention to the times of transition on your journey. Wayne Oates provides a grid for evaluating your turning points: "These times of transition may be of two kinds—emergency transitions or developmental transitions."[6] Emergency transitions include illness, death, divorce, voluntary job loss, or even involuntary job termination. In these situations, you can find comfort from the voluntary job loss of John Mark, from the involuntary job termination of Barnabas, from the temporary blindness of Paul, and from the unexpected death of Stephen. In contrast to the finality of bereavement associated with death and dying, Wayne Oates describes these traumatic forms of loss as "grief in the face of life" (Acts 15:35-41):

> What grief Barnabas must have felt! What lonely feelings of estrangement Paul must have felt! Now each of them was on his own . . . the relationship between [Paul] and Barnabas, the man who gave him his start in the Christian community, apparently was never the same again. The infection apparently departed and the wound healed but the scar tissues probably remained.[7]

The same acute grief process is found in Pastor Betty's experience with fire-bombing. Furthermore, Augustine wrote the *Confessions* in the wake of an emergency situation—the death of his mother—and Wayne Oates' autobiography includes a painful crisis experience—the lack of recognition as a certified CPE supervisor. Since all of these stories involve an emergency of one kind or another, it is not likely that your ministry formation will be devoid of problems or disappointments.

Viewing these stories as developmental experiences is the other way of looking at your transitions. Your age at the beginning of your ministry will determine whether your first developmental crisis takes place at the point of entry, mid-life, or pre-retirement. Paul's ministry began with an entry crisis of dramatic conversion. John Mark began his ministry with a normative identity crisis. Stephen did not get beyond his entry crisis, however, because of a misjudgment of the intensity of his opposition. Peter modeled the need for continuing conversion in mid-life beyond his initial entry into ministry. Augustine successfully negotiated his mid-life crisis by making a career change from secular public oratory to a Christian pulpit ministry. Wayne Oates successfully negotiated his entry crisis by overcoming a roadblock to his early teaching career.

Emergency and developmental transitions will be an important part of your journey. The previous biblical, historical, and contemporary stories will help you to deal with both unexpected traumas and anticipated changes. These unavoidable times of transition will hold in store for you what James Loder calls "revelatory moments" or what Robert Havighurst calls "teachable moments." Monitoring them carefully will help you to understand the sudden turning points of your ministry formation. You will also want to keep an eye out for one more rail marker.

PERSIST IN YOUR SEARCH

Your persistence as a pilgrim will provide you with a wealth of experience to share when the time comes for you to consider the art of spiritual companionship. The strength that develops in your pastoral identity of "mind, soul, and will" becomes the reservoir from which you will draw during the times of transition. You will anticipate the movement from being led by a mentor to becoming a mentor yourself when your story can be shared on the way as a resource for a fellow pilgrim.

For some persons, like myself, the task of spiritual nurturing may be most natural after you have entered mid-life; it may come sooner for others. The focus of this book has been on your entry crisis, which sets the direction for at least the first decade of your professional development. An emphasis on your own spiritual formation will prepare you to become a spiritual companion whenever you are ready to begin discipling someone else.

A poster that portrays a pathway in the midst of a dense forest has a provocative caption: "If you don't know where you are going, any path will do." Does your approach to ministry formation include a determination to persist on the pathway that will lead you toward the goal of becoming a spiritual companion? Two additional captions will be added to this poster. They will help you to find your way toward the desired goal of effective leadership.

Persistence suggests that you *keep both feet on the ground.* Your own spiritual journey is not an ethereal escape into mysticism, but an awareness of God's presence in the everyday events of your ministry. Wayne Oates calls it "down-to-earth centering [through which] you value silence as the collecting point of your whole being."[8] It will enable you to discover "the pure gold of God" in yourself and in the events that shape your ministry. Your inner life needs to be connected with down-to-earth concerns of ordinary people and institutions. Your talk about spirituality will be grounded in the reality of daily life and world events. Spirituality does not need to drift into the nebulous realm outside or above this world in order to be significant.

Persistence also requires you to *invite a spiritual friend to walk with you.* President John A. Mackay left an indelible impression on me as a new doctoral candidate at Princeton Theological Seminary. One sentence captures the essence of his wide-reaching churchmanship: "We become related to Christ singly, but we cannot live in Christ solitarily."[9] The formative years at the beginning of your ministry will be much more rewarding if your experience of living "in Christ" includes a spiritual friend who will walk with you on the same path. It may be a fellow minister or a special acquaintance in the congregation (or other ministry context). Moving from a peer relationship to the privilege of becoming a spiritual companion will be the next step.

Your ministry formation may have begun in the roller coaster pattern of John Mark. Yet, your journey points ahead to a straight pathway on which you can walk with a spiritual friend. It leads to the goal of nurturing "a son [or daughter] of encouragement," such as Barnabas.[10] Your uniqueness as a growing minister and a future spiritual companion may be more like the empathetic orientation of Peter, the efficient orientation of Stephen, or the effective orientation of Paul. The particular strength you bring to the ministry will equip you, like Pastor Betty, to rise to the challenge of any transitional crisis that comes your way. Your own pastoral identity, like that of Augustine, will emerge from this struggle "to do" God's will and "to be" God's person. The journey itself will enrich your life, like Wayne Oates, with a variety of experiences that will shape your spiritual formation.

The only story that remains to be told is your own. I have developed elsewhere a reflective process for discovering, evoking, completing, and interpreting life stories.[11] The sharing of your personal identity narratives will enrich spiritual companionship. These stories from your childhood and youth also can be used to focus theological and self-reflection upon the issues of ministry formation.

Your ministry formation is not achieved once and for all. Instead, you continually approach it through a sensitive openness to balancing personhood and performance. Do not even think about putting this book aside without a commitment to seek out a spiritual friend or to express appreciation for the one you already have. This self-help manual will provide the two of you with a road map for the mutual exploration of your limitations, your style of leadership, and your spiritual formation. You are on the way to growing awareness, increasing competence, and deepening satisfaction in ministry.[12] This formation process will become the vision that will guide your journey for the rest of your life. The use of a daily devotional guide will help you to keep that vision in sharp focus.

> And you, too, youthful reader, will realize the Vision (not the idle wish) of your heart, be it base or beautiful, or a mixture of both, for you will always gravitate toward that which you, secretly, most love. Into your hands will be placed the exact results of your own thoughts; you will receive that which you earn; no more, no less. Whatever your present

> environment may be, you will fall, remain, or rise with your thoughts, your Vision, your Ideal. You will become as small as your controlling desire; as great as your dominant aspiration. . . .
>
> "Gifts," powers, material, intellectual, and spiritual possessions are the fruits of effort; they are thoughts completed, objects accomplished, visions realized.
>
> The vision that you glorify in your mind, the Ideal that you enthrone in your heart—this you will build your life by, this you will become.[13]

With God's help and the encouragement of a spiritual friend, you are ready to become your own supervisor or overseer. You are invited back to the balcony in order to get a bird's eye view of your journey on the road. Then, the direction you choose as a traveler will be informed by your own "super-vision" for ministry.

NOTES

INTRODUCTION

1. Doran McCarty, *Supervising Ministry Students,* rev. ed. (Atlanta: Home Missions Board, Southern Baptist Convention, 1986), p. 9.

2. Luke is cited as the author of Luke-Acts without debating the various theories of authorship, which are beyond the scope of this study.

1. IDENTIFYING YOUR LIMITATIONS: *JOHN MARK*

1. The Greek word *hypērétēs* literally means "an underrower" and is used as the title for a physician's aid, a Roman consul's aid, and an assistant to a religious cult leader. Luke's usage is equivalent to the Hebrew word *chazzen,* which signifies the only paid employee in the synagogue, who is not only the instructor in the Scriptures for the synagogue school but also is the janitor (see Luke 4:20).

2. Eusebius, *Ecclesiastical History,* 3. 39. 15.

3. Frank Stagg, *The Book of Acts: The Early Struggle for an Unhindered Gospel* (Nashville: Broadman Press, 1955), p. 140.

4. Clarence Jordan, *The Cotton Patch Version of Luke and Acts: Jesus' Doings and the Happenings* (New York: Association Press, 1969), p. 121, describes in a rare footnote the way in which Paul confronts Bar-Jesus as "sharp and brutal . . . giving evidence that even saints like Paul, especially young, fresh ones, may come unglued and lose their cool."

5. Eric H. Erikson, *Childhood and Society*, 2nd rev. ed. (New York: W. W. Norton Co., 1963), pp. 247-74.

6. Eric H. Erikson, *Identity: Youth and Crisis* (New York: W. W. Norton & Co., 1968), p. 212.

7. Carol Gilligan, *In a Different Voice: Psychological Theory and Women's Development* (Cambridge, Mass.: Harvard University Press, 1982), p. 12; see pp. 261-94.

8. James W. Fowler, *Stages of Faith: The Psychology of Human Development and the Quest for Meaning* (New York: Harper & Row, 1981), pp. 117-213. The sixth stage, Universalizing Faith, will be omitted because it is a goal that is attained by fewer persons, such as Dag Hammerskjöld or Martin Luther King, Jr.

9. Thomas A. Droege, *Faith Passages and Patterns* (Philadelphia: Fortress Press, 1983), pp. 44-63; makes the technical language of Fowler (see parenthetical terminology) more comprehensible to the average reader.

10. Rollo May, *Power and Innocence* (New York: W. W. Norton & Co., 1972), p. 100.

11. H. Richard Niebuhr, *The Meaning of Revelation* (New York: Macmillan, 1941), p. 36.

12. Ibid., pp. 59-66, esp. 60.

13. Roger C. Palms, *God Holds Your Tomorrows* (Minneapolis: Augsburg Publishing House, 1976), p. 66.

2. RECOGNIZING YOUR UNIQUENESS: *PETER, STEPHEN, AND PAUL*

1. Ernest Haenchen, *The Acts of the Apostles: A Commentary* (Philadelphia: The Westminster Press, 1971), p. 103. Luke's special technique of presenting history in the form of stories is recognized by Haenchen: "Luke firmly believed that the history of Christian beginnings was edifying in itself, but to present it as such he had to employ a special technique and offer his readers history in the guise of stories." In relation to ancient history, Luke's literary style is more like the storytelling manner of Herodotus than the factual chronicles of Thucydides.

2. Raymond E. Brown, Karl P. Donfried, and John Reuman, eds., *Peter in the New Testament* (Minneapolis: Augsburg Publishing House, 1973), pp. 40-42.

3. Ernst Haenchen observes: "It was in other words no 'freelance' who began the mission to the Gentiles, but the legitimate, apostolic Church" (*Acts of the Apostles*, p. 360). Luke is making this point both historically and theologically.

4. The chronic bereavement process of Elizabeth Kübler-Ross (*On Death and Dying* [New York: Macmillan, 1969]) fits Peter's situation better than the acute process of Erich Lindemann, "Symptomatology and Management of Acute Grief" (*American Journal of Psychiatry* 101 [1944], pp. 141-48), which is cited by Wayne E. Oates (*Anxiety in Christian Experience* [Philadelphia: The Westminster Press, 1955], p. 51).

5. Amos N. Wilder's discussion of the power of poetics helps to explain Peter's angry reaction: "We should recognize that human nature and human societies are more deeply motivated by images . . . than by ideas." *Theopoetics: Theology and Religious Imagination* (Philadelphia: Fortress Press, 1976), p. 2.

6. Morton Kelsey, *Companions on the Inner Way: The Art of Spiritual Guidance* (New York: Crossroads, 1984), describes the bargaining aspect of an important dream, which involved a large and wise-looking turtle knocking three times at a stone cliff. He reports that for two years, several hours each month were spent exploring this inner world that the turtle revealed. Likewise, the bargaining surely continued in Peter's mind, following his trance-vision (p. 141).

7. Ernst Haenchen affirms: "By the end of the story the reader will no longer forget that it *was* God who brought about the whole of these events: and thereby instituted the mission to the Gentiles" (*Acts of the Apostles*, p. 358).

8. F. F. Bruce, *Peter, Stephen, James, and John: Studies in Non-Pauline Christianity* (Grand Rapids: W. B. Eerdmans Publishing Co., 1979), p. 36.

9. Walter Eichrodt, *Theology of the Old Testament*, vol. 1 (Philadelphia: The Westminster Press, 1961), p. 392; identifies the priests as "the official functionaries of the worship of Yahweh." Peter, as the spokesman of the twelve, is certainly the first official functionary of the Jerusalem church.

10. The technical terms from the Myers-Briggs Type Indicator describe my personality profile as extroverted—intuitive/feeling—judging (ENFJ). The latter term refers to the ability to make decisions easily. The inner traits refer to *being* and the outer ones to *doing*. An easy way to learn your profile is to use the simplified questionnaire developed by David Keirsey and Marilyn Bates, *Please Understand Me: Character and Temperment Types* (Del Mar, Calif: Prometheus Nemesis Books, 1978), pp. 5-11. Your interpretation of the results will be aided by Isabel Briggs Myers, *Gifts Differing* (Palo Alto, Calif.: Consulting Psychologists Press, 1980).

11. William R. Myers, "Spiritual Formation: A Quest for Wholeness." *ATS Notes* (December 1984/January 1985) 1-2.

12. David W. Augsburger, *Anger and Assertiveness in Pastoral Care* (Philadelphia: Fortress Press, 1979), pp. 38-49.

13. Morton Kelsey insists: "The blind cannot lead the blind. An analyst can help others only after being helped, and the spiritual director only by having been directed" (*The Christian and the Supernatural* [Minneapolis: Augsburg Publishing House, 1976], p. 158).

14. Brevard S. Childs, *Old Testament Theology in a Canonical Context* (Philadelphia: Fortress Press, 1985), insists: "The prophets stood in a long history of tradition on which they were dependent. The original prophets were primarily proclaimers rather than authors—forthtellers not fore-tellers—who couched their oracles in traditional, stereotyped speech forms" (p. 122). This perspective accurately describes Stephen's use of the history of Israel in his "forthtelling" of the Gentile mission.

15. Ernst Haenchen affirms: "For if Jesus stands on the right hand of God, this must show that the Christians are right in the sight of God and that the High Council is virtually God's enemy" (*Acts of the Apostles*, p. 295).

16. Haenchen, *Acts of the Apostles*, p. 365, note 5.

17. H. Richard Niebuhr, *Meaning of Revelation*, p. 113. Uses these expressions as translations of the word *repentance* (*metanoia*) which describes the "permanent revolution" or the ongoing transformation of human life under divine initiative: "God's self-disclosure is that permanent revolution in our religious life by which all religious truths are painfully transformed and all religious behavior transfigured by *repentance* and new faith."

18. Krister Stendahl, *Paul Among Jews and Greeks* (Philadelphia: Fortress Press, 1976), pp. 7-23; suggests that Paul accepts his mission as a Jew who is specifically commissioned to reach the Gentiles for Christ (Acts 25:16-19): "The mission

is the point . . . it is obvious that Paul remains a Jew as he fulfills his role as an Apostle to the Gentiles" (pp. 10-11). Technically, Paul remains a Jew, but the encounter with Christ makes him a believer or follower even though the term "Christian" is not yet in common usage.

19. James E. Loder, *The Transforming Moment: Understanding Convictional Experiences* (New York: Harper & Row, 1981), p. 37.

20. Ibid, p. 6.

21. Ibid., p. 15.

22. Morton Kelsey, *Dreams: A Way to Listen to God* (New York: Paulist Press, 1978), p. 17.

23. Walter Eichrodt, *Theology of the Old Testament*, vol. 1 (Philadelphia: The Westminster Press, 1961), pp. 442-56; suggests that the concept of kingship in Israel was distinct from the Canaanite conception. The Israelite idea of king was vested with a "religious aura," which combined the charismatic role of prophet and the official role of priest. The Canaanite king was merely invested with the authority to govern.

24. A useful roadmap in this regard is *Heirs of the Same Promise: Using Acts as a Study Guide for Evangelizing Ethnic America*. Edited by Wesley D. Balda (Arcadia, Calif.: National Convocation on Evangelizing Ethnic America, 1984).

25. Lyle E. Schaller, *Assimilating New Members* (Nashville: Abingdon Press, 1978), p. 78.

26. William R. Nelson and William F. Lincoln, *Journey Toward Renewal* (Valley Forge, Pa.: Judson Press, 1971), pp. 26, 53.

27. See note 10 above. Another scheme for evaluating the

interaction of leadership styles is presented by Robert Dale, *Pastoral Leadership* (Nashville: Abingdon Press, 1986), pp. 39-54.

3. TESTING YOUR PASTORAL LEADERSHIP: *BETTY HOCHSTETLER*

1. Betty Hochstetler, "A Church Renewed By Fire." *The SCUPE Report*, vol. 4, no. 1 (February, 1982) 2-4.

2. Ralph Neighbour, *The Seven Last Words of the Church* (Grand Rapids: Zondervan, 1973), pp. 15-19.

3. Lyle E. Schaller, *Effective Church Planning* (Nashville: Abingdon Press, 1979), p. 120.

4. Lloyd John Ogilvie, *Drumbeat of Love: The Unlimited Power of the Spirit as Revealed in the Book of Acts* (Waco, Tex.: Word Books, 1976), p. 101.

5. Roland Allan, *The Spontaneous Expansion of the Church and the Causes Which Hinder It* (London: World Dominion Press, 1949), pp. 6-17.

6. C. Peter Wagner, *Our Kind of People: The Ethical Dimensions of Church Growth in America* (Atlanta: John Knox Press, 1979); presents a strong case for "the homogeneous unit principle," a basic tenet of the Church Growth movement. This strategy of uniformity is challenged by the demonstration of unity in diversity throughout the book of Acts. See Ralph H. Elliott, "Dangers of the Church Growth Movement." *Christian Century* (August 12-19, 1981) 799-801, and *Church Growth That Counts* (Valley Forge, Pa.: Judson Press, 1982), pp. 53-88.

7. Schaller, *Assimilating New Members*, pp. 78-79.

8. Lee Hochstetler's personality profile is introverted—intuitive/feeling—judging (INFJ). His inner being of intuition and feeling would make him a sensitive minister with an aging congregation. His soft touch of introversion and his ease of decision-making would keep him in touch with both the congregation and the community.

9. Schaller, *Assimilating New Members*, pp. 76-77.

10. Ibid., pp. 76 and 78.

11. Pastor Betty's personality traits are ESFJ (extroverted-sensing/feeling-judging). Her outgoing emotional sensitivity (EF) is in tension with her sensible approach to decision-making (SJ).

12. Arlin J. Rothauge, *Sizing up a Congregation for New Member Ministry* (New York: The Episcopal Church Center, 1983), p. 5. This typology works in most cases, but needs to be qualified by the atypical personality of some congregations. A congregation of 100 members, which is dominated by professional persons, would function like a Program Church. A congregation of 100 members in a rural area or one dominated by blue-collar persons would still function like a Family Church.

13. George G. Hunter, III, *The Contagious Congregation: Frontiers in Evangelism and Church Growth* (Nashville: Abingdon Press, 1979), pp. 35-63.

4. INTEGRATING YOUR PASTORAL IDENTITY: *AUGUSTINE*

1. *The Confessions of St. Augustine.* Translated by John K. Ryan (Garden City, N. Y.: Image Books, 1960), pp. 55-57. Roman numerals for books I to XIII will be cited along with the Arabic subsections without the chapter numbers between.

2. Robert J. O'Connell, *St. Augustine's Confessions: The Odyssey of the Soul* (Cambridge, Mass.: Harvard University Press, 1969), pp. 5-22.

3. Peter Brown, *Augustine of Hippo: A Biography* (Berkeley, Calif.: University of California Press, 1967).

4. H. Richard Niebuhr and D. D. Williams, eds. *The Ministry in Historical Perspective* (New York: Harper and Bros., 1956). Traces the beginning of seminaries, in the modern sense to the higher education needs of the Roman Catholic Church in 1530. Modern Protestant seminaries date from the early nineteenth century, beginning with General Theological Seminary, which was founded by the Episcopal Church in New York City in 1819.

5. Joseph B. Bernadin, "St. Augustine as Pastor." In Roy W. Battenhouse, ed. *A Companion to the Study of St. Augustine* (Grand Rapids: Baker Book House, 1955), pp. 57-89, esp. p. 59.

6. H. Richard Niebuhr, *The Purpose of the Church and Its Ministry* (New York: Harper and Bros., 1956), p. 64. See Charles W. Stewart, *Person and Profession: Career Development in the Ministry* (Nashville: Abingdon Press, 1974), pp. 21-41.

7. Charles H. Chandler, "What About Pastoral Support Groups?" *Church Administration* (January, 1983) 6-30; (February, 1983) 23-31; and (March, 1983), pp. 29-31.

8. Paul W. Pruyser, "Psychological Examination: Augustine." *Journal for the Scientific Study of Religion* 5 (1965-66) 284-89; and Donald E. Capps, "The Parabolic Event in Religious Autobiography." *Princeton Seminary Bulletin*, IV-1 (1983) 26-38. See Donald Capps, *Life Cycle Theory and Pastoral Care* (Philadelphia: Fortress Press, 1983), pp. 81-98.

9. Donald E. Capps, *Princeton Seminary Bulletin*, IV-1 (1983) 34.

10. Wayne E. Oates, *Christ and Selfhood* (New York: Association Press, 1961), pp. 220-22.

11. William Glasser, *Stations of the Mind: New Directions for Reality Therapy* (New York: Harper & Row, 1981), pp. 238-39; uses the psychological categories of thinking, feeling, and doing, which are foreshadowed in Augustine's mind, soul/heart, and will.

12. Brown, *Augustine of Hippo*, pp. 287-98, 381-97.

13. Richard Dyer, "Though Conducting Always His Goal, Conlon Slowed Tempo to Get There." *Chicago Tribune*, Section 13 (July 21, 1985) 24.

14. James Glasse, *Putting It Together in the Parish* (Nashville: Abingdon Press, 1972), pp. 53-61.

15. Richard J. Foster, *Celebration of Discipline: The Path to Spiritual Growth* (San Francisco: Harper & Row, 1978) and Richard J. Foster, *Study Guide for Celebration of Discipline* (San Francisco: Harper & Row, 1983).

16. Petrarch, *De contemptu mundi*, Dial 1. Cited in E. Glen Hinson, *Seekers After Mature Faith: A Historical Introduction to the Classics of Christian Devotion*, with special psychological commentary by Wayne E. Oates (Waco, Tex.: Word Books, 1968), pp. 44-45.

17. Brown, *Augustine of Hippo*, p. 202.

18. R. L. Ottley, *Studies in the Confessions of Augustine* (London: Paternoster Row, 1919), p. 109.

5. ACCELERATING YOUR SPIRITUAL FORMATION: *WAYNE E. OATES*

1. Wayne E. Oates, *The Struggle to Be Free: My Story and Your Story* (Philadelphia: The Westminster Press, 1983). The

primary source for the summary of his story. See Gerald L. Borchert and Andrew D. Lester, eds. *Spiritual Dimensions of Pastoral Care: Witness to the Ministry of Wayne E. Oates* (Philadelphia: The Westminster Press, 1985), the *Festschrift* growing out of the Wayne E. Oates Festival on April 2-4, 1984, in Louisville, Kentucky.

2. Denise George, "Wayne E. Oates: The Father of Pastoral Care." *Western Recorder* (December 21, 1983) 7.

3. Wayne E. Oates and Charles E. Oates, M.D., *People in Pain: Guidelines for Pastoral Care* (Philadelphia: The Westminster Press, 1985).

4. Wayne E. Oates, *The Struggle to Be Free*, p. 60. Among his most important works is the first of a trilogy of writings, which develops his trinitarian theology: *Protestant Pastoral Counseling* (Philadelphia: The Westminster Press, 1962). This out-of-print volume has been followed by a twenty-four-years-later sequel called *The Presence of God in Pastoral Counseling* (Waco, Tex.: Word Books, 1986).

5. Oates, *The Struggle to Be Free*, p. 59; cf. pp. 95-96.

6. Edward E. Thornton, "Presentation of the Distinguished Service Award to Wayne Edward Oates." *1983 ACPE Conference Proceedings* (New York: Association for Clinical Pastoral Education, 1984) 43. The verbal presentation was made on October 14, 1983, in Portland, Maine.

7. Edward E. Thornton, *Professional Education for Ministry: A History of Clinical Pastoral Education* (Nashville: Abingdon Press, 1970), p. 154.

8. Oates, *The Struggle to Be Free*, p. 97.

9. Ibid., pp. 97-98.

10. Wayne E Oates, *The Significance of the Work of Sigmund*

Freud for the Christian Faith (Unpublished doctoral thesis. Louisville, Ky., The Southern Baptist Theological Seminary, 1947).

11. Wayne E. Oates, "The Ecumenical Thrust of Clinical Pastoral Education." An Address Delivered at the Association of Clinical Pastoral Education Meeting, October 16, 1967. (Unpublished manuscript. Louisville, Ky.: Southern Baptist Theological Seminary), pp. 3 and 7.

12. Wayne E. Oates, *Life's Detours* (Nashville: The Upper Room, 1974), pp. 9, 79-80.

13. Ibid., pp. 56-57. See Anton Boisen, *The Exploration of the Inner World: A Study of Mental Disorder and Religious Experience* (Chicago: Willett, Clark, & Co., 1936. Reprinted twice by New York: Harper and Bros., 1952, and Philadelphia: University of Pennsylvania Press, 1971) and *Problems in Religion and Life: A Manual for Pastors* (Nashville: Abingdon-Cokesbury Press, 1946).

14. Thornton, *Professional Education for Ministry*, p. 153.

15. Oates, *Life's Detours*, p. 85.

16. Oates, *The Struggle to Be Free*, pp. 119-20.

17. Brown, *Augustine of Hippo*, p. 87; see pp. 408-9.

18. Oates, *The Struggle to Be Free*, p. 51.

19. Wayne E. Oates, "Organizational Development and Pastoral Care." *Review and Expositor*, LXXV-3 (Summer, 1978) 349-360, esp. 349.

20. See Oates, *The Struggle to Be Free*, p. 98.

21. William A. Barry and William J. Connolly, *The Practice of Spiritual Direction* (New York: Seabury Press, 1982); L. Patrick

Carroll and Katharine Marie Dyckman, *Inviting the Mystic, Supporting the Prophet: An Introduction to Spiritual Direction* (New York: Paulist Press, 1981); Tilden H. Edwards, *Spiritual Friend: Reclaiming the Gift of Spiritual Direction* (New York: Paulist Press, 1980); Morton T. Kelsey, *Companions on the Inner Way: The Art of Spiritual Guidance* (New York: Crossroad, 1984); Kenneth Leech, *Experiencing God: Theology as Spirituality* (San Francisco: Harper & Row, 1985) and *Soul Friend: The Practice of Christian Spirituality* (San Francisco: Harper & Row, 1980); Ignatius Loyola, *The Spiritual Exercises.* Translated by Anthony Mottola (New York: Image Books, 1958); Thomas Merton, *Spiritual Direction and Meditation* (Collegeville, Minn.: Liturgical Press, 1960); August Nebe, *Luther* as *Spiritual Advisor*. Translated by C. A. Hay and C. E. Hay (Philadelphia: Fortress Press, 1894); Henri J. M. Nouwen, *Reaching Out: The Three Movements of the Spiritual Life* (Garden City, N. Y.: Doubleday, 1975); Edward E. Thornton, *Being Transformed: An Inner Way of Spiritual Growth* (Philadelphia: The Westminster Press, 1984); W. Walsh, "Reality Therapy and Spiritual Direction." *Review for Religions,* vol. 35 (1976), pp. 372-85; John Welch, *Spiritual Pilgrims: Carl Jung and Theresa of Avila* (New York: Paulist Press, 1982); and J. H. Wright, "A Discussion of Spiritual Direction." *Studies in the Spirituality of Jesuits,* IV-2 (March, 1972) 1-51. See Susanne Johnson, "Selected Bibliography on Spirituality, Formation and Direction." *Spirituality, Ministry and Field Education—Theological Field Education Key Resources,* vol. 5, ed. by Donald F. Beisswenger, Doran C. McCarty, and Lynn Rhodes (The Association for Theological Field Education, Copyright Dr. Doran C. McCarty, 1986) 64-82.

22. Oates, *The Struggle to Be Free,* p. 87. See Wayne E. Oates, *Nurturing Silence in a Noisy Heart* (Garden City, N. Y.: Doubleday and Co., 1979) and Basil Pennington, *The Centering Prayer* (Garden City, N. Y.: Doubleday and Co., 1980).

23. Oates, *The Struggle to Be Free,* pp. 20-21.

24. Ibid. p. 41.

25. Ibid., pp. 50-51.

26. Wayne E. Oates, *Confessions of a Workaholic: The Facts About Work Addiction* (New York: World Publications, 1971). See Wayne E. Oates, *Your Right to Rest* (Philadelphia: The Westminster Press, 1984).

27. John H. McClanahan, "Book Review of Wayne E. Oates, *The Struggle to Be Free.*" *Review and Expositor,* LXXXI-3 (Summer, 1984) 488-89. See John H. McClanahan, *The Psychology of the Self in the Writings of Augustine* (Unpublished doctoral thesis. Louisville, Ky.: Southern Baptist Theological Seminary, 1957).

28. Wayne E. Oates, *The Christian Pastor,* 3rd ed., rev. (Philadelphia: The Westminster Press, 1982), pp. 190-218, can be adapted as the levels of spiritual formation: (1) friendship, (2) comfort, (3) confession, and (4) instruction.

29. Wayne E. Oates, *Christ and Selfhood* (New York: Association Press, 1961), pp. 22, 32. Italics added. This least known of Oates' major works is dedicated to his first mentor, Olin T. Binkley. It is the second volume in his trinitarian trilogy (see note 4 above). The third work is Wayne E. Oates, *The Holy Spirit in Five Worlds: The Psychedelic, the Nonverbal, the Articulate, the New Morality, the Administrative* (New York: Association Press, 1960).

30. Oates, *Christ and Selfhood,* pp. 22, 26. Italics added.

31. Ibid., pp. 22, 25.

32. Ibid., pp. 45, 91; see pp. 22, 42, and 133.

33. Oates, *The Struggle to Be Free,* p. 85.

34. John H. McClanahan, *Review and Expositor,* LXXXI-3

(Summer, 1984) 489. See Wayne E. Oates, "Pastoral Supervision Today." *Pastoral Psychology*, vol. 24 (Fall, 1975) 17-29.

35. William Malcomson, *Success Is a Failure Experience: Male Liberation and the American Myth of Success* (Nashville: Abingdon Press, 1976).

36. Oates, *Nurturing Silence in a Noisy Heart*, pp. 15, 99.

37. Oates, *The Struggle to be Free*, p. 162.

CONCLUSION

1. John A. Mackay, *A Preface to Christian Theology* (New York: Macmillan, 1941), pp. 27-54.

2. Dag Hammarskjöld, *Markings* (New York: Ballantine Books, 1964). Models the need for "trail marks" that you can record in your own spiritual diary or journal. See Morton F. Kelsey, *Adventure Inward: Christian Growth Through Personal Journal Writing* (Minneapolis: Augsburg Publishing House, 1980); Ira Progoff, *At a Journal Workshop* (New York: Dialogue House Library, 1975); and George F. Simons, *Keeping Your Spiritual Journal* (New York: Paulist Press, 1978).

3. H. Richard Niebuhr, *The Meaning of Revelation* (New York: Macmillan, 1941), p. 100.

4. Ibid.

5. Timothy George, "Seminary Career Likened to 'Pilgrimage.' " *The Towers* (Louisville, Ky.: Southern Baptist Theological Seminary) II-4 (September 10, 1984), 3.

6. Wayne E. Oates, *When Religion Gets Sick* (Philadelphia: The Westminster Press, 1970), p. 84.

7. Wayne E. Oates, *Anxiety in Christian Experience* (Philadelphia: The Westminster Press, 1955), p. 56.

8. Wayne E. Oates, *Nurturing Silence in a Noisy Heart* (Garden City, N. Y.: Doubleday, 1979), p. 43.

9. John A. Mackay, *God's Order: The Ephesian Letter and This Present Time* (London: James Nisbet & Co., 1953), p. 148.

10. Jeanne Doering, *The Power of Encouragement: Discovering Your Ministry of Affirmation* (Chicago: Moody Press, 1982).

11. William R. Nelson, "A Narrative Approach to Theological Reflection," *Journal of Supervision and Training in Ministry*, vol. 9 (1987); part of a symposium on Story Theology and Ministry Supervision.

12. William E. Hulme, Milo L. Brekke, and William C. Behrens, *Pastors in Ministry: Guidelines for Seven Critical Issues* (Minneapolis: Augsburg Publishing House, 1985). Presents the findings of an empirical research projct with 1,200 ministers, mostly Lutherans, in various stages of ministry formation. The seven critical issues are: (1) achieving competence and satisfaction in ministerial functions; (2) deepening the spiritual/devotional life; (3) developing the potential of clergy marriages; (4) learning to live within limits; (5) overcoming an adversarial role toward the congregation, (6) utilizing opportunities for friendship, retreat, and corporate support; and (7) improving the health of parish ministry. The majority of these issues have been identified intuitively by reflecting on biblical, historical, and contemporary stories. Those issues that you have not yet faced in this list will suggest what lies ahead during the second decade of your ministry formation.

13. James Allen, *As a Man Thinketh* (Old Tappan, N. J.: Fleming H. Revell Co., n.d.), quoted in Reuben P. Job and Norman Shawchuck, *A Guide to Prayer for Ministers and Other Servants* (Nashville: The Upper Room, 1983), p. 272.

ADDITIONAL RESOURCES

The Rev. Duane Parker, Executive Director
Association for Clinical Pastoral Education, Inc. (ACPE)
1549 Clairmont Road, Suite 103
Decatur, Georgia 30033
(404) 320-1472

Dr. Lynn Rhodes, Chairperson
Carol J. Allen, Treasurer
Association for Theological Field Education (ATFE)
5555 South Woodlawn Avenue
Chicago, Illinois 60637
(312) 241-7800

Dr. Ira Progoff, Director; June Gordon, Associate Director
Dialogue House: National Intensive Journal Program
80 East 11th Street
New York, New York 10003
(212) 673-5881

Marjory Zoet Bankson, President
Faith at Work, Inc.
11065 Little Patuxent Parkway
Columbia, Maryland 21044
(301) 730-3690

Dr. Win Arn, President
The Institute for American Church Growth
709 East Colorado Boulevard, Suite 150
Pasadena, California 91101
(818) 449-4400

Tom Warren, Executive Director
Institute for Christian Ministry
354 Franklin Street
Mansfield, Maine 02048
(617) 339-6466

Mrs. Betsy Edwards, Director
The Institute of Spiritual Companionship
3320 Robincrest Drive
Northbrook, Illinois 60062
(312) 489-1342 or 523-7744

George A. Fitchett, Editor
Journal of Supervision and Training in Ministry
P. O. Box 6777
Chicago, Illinois 60680
(312) 942-5571

The Rev. L. Ronald Brushwyler, Executive Director
Midwest Career Development Service
1840 Westchester Boulevard
P. O. Box 7249
Westchester, Illinois 60153
(312) 343-6268

2501 North Star Road, Suite 200
Columbus, Ohio 43221
(614) 486-0469

National Convocation on Evangelizing
American Mission Advanced Research and Communication Center
(MARC)
P. O. Box 3137
Arcadia, California 91006

Dr. David J. Frenchak, Executive Director
Seminary Consortium for Urban Pastoral Education (SCUPE)
30 West Chicago Avenue
Chicago, Illinois 60610
(312) 944-2153

Dr. Patricia Cremins, Executive Secretary
The Society for the Advancement of Continuing Education for Ministry (SACEM)
228 Auerbach Hall
University of Hartford
Hartford, Connecticut 06117
(202) 243-4350